"Wow, what a tool to create a ... thing you need to create a ...
—C...

D0020963

P7—EVP—854

Coach Yourself

to a New Career

7 Steps to Reinventing Your Professional Life

....

TALANE MIEDANER

New York Chicago San Francisco Lisbon London Madrid Mexico City
Milan New Delhi San Juan Seoul Singapore Sydney Toronto

Library of Congress Cataloging-in-Publication Data

Miedaner, Talane.
    Coach yourself to a new career : 7 steps to reinventing your professional life / by Talane
    Miedaner.
            p.   cm.
    Includes index.
    ISBN-13: 978-0-07-170309-3
    ISBN-10: 0-07-170309-8
    1. Career changes.   2. Career development.   3. Success in business.

HF5384.M544   2010
650.14—dc22   2009039624

1 2 3 4 5 6 7 8 9 10 11 12 13 14 15 16 17 18   DOC/DOC   1 9 8 7 6 5 4 3 2 1 0

ISBN 978-0-07-170309-3
MHID   0-07-170309-8

Interior design by THINK Book Works

McGraw-Hill books are available at special quantity discounts to use as premiums and sales
promotions or for use in corporate training programs. To contact a representative, please e-mail
us at bulksales@mcgraw-hill.com.

The instructions and advice in this book are not intended as a substitute for psychological
counseling. The author and the publisher disclaim any responsibility or liability resulting from the
actions advocated or discussed in this book. In the interest of preserving client confidentiality, all
clients' names and, in some cases, identifying characteristics have been changed except where
permission to use first and last names has been granted. The scenarios, situations, and results
are real.

To Paul, my knight in shining armor

Contents

Acknowledgments

With tremendous gratitude and appreciation, I'd like to thank the following people:

Mom, once again, you are and always have been the most supportive person of my writing. A thousand thanks for getting up at the crack of dawn with the girls all summer so that I could use the mornings to either sleep or write. And a very special thank-you to my sister Keralee, who was not only the chief chef and bottle washer but also the beloved laundry fairy and a wonderful aunt to the girls so that I could happily ignore the details of domestic life and focus on writing. I honestly don't think I did anything other than scramble an egg or two all summer long, thanks to you two wonderfully supportive angels!

Fiona Sarne, the brilliant editor at McGraw-Hill who worked most closely with me on the finer details of the book. Not only do I appreciate all your insightful comments and suggestions that most certainly improved the book, but also and more than anything I appreciate your cheerful enthusiasm, which made it a fun and effortless (well, almost!) project. It has been a pleasure working with you. Emily Carleton for your excellent ideas and comments and working with me to get the right structure in place, and Judith McCarthy, my publisher at McGraw-Hill, for inviting me to write the book in the first place and making it possible. Charlie Fisher and his production team for making the book look great; the marketing and publicity team, especially Heather Cooper and Staci Shands; and Sally Ashworth, Maya Barahona, and Sue Blake in the UK office. It has always been a pleasure working with the very professional team at McGraw-Hill.

My sister Sarelyn for your ongoing e-mail and phone support and for your wonderfully witty sense of humor. You always make me laugh at the oddest of things, which reminds me not to take life so seriously.

Vic, Dale, and Logan Bosiger for welcoming me into your home and hearts. Vic, you have been and continue to be one of my biggest fans, and I deeply appreciate all the support you've so generously given to promote the book with the radio show and all your help with Lifecoach.com and a thousand other things. I thank my lucky stars that you are a part of my life. Logan, thanks for all your help in getting me up on Facebook.

The extraordinary team of coaches at Talane Coaching Company—Judy Lowry, Kathee Hill, Monica Howden, Sue Seel, Eddie Marmol, and Terry O'Neill—for all your ideas and input that led to the creation of the original Emotional Index Quiz. Judy, thank you for all your excellent coaching and your enthusiastic support of everything that I undertake. And a big, huge thank-you to Faye Morgan, my wonderful and ever-positive assistant. I'd be lost without your help with all things administrative. Thanks to Louise Gates, Lea Wray, and Carol Golcher as well for your help with all things organizational and administrative.

The late Thomas Leonard, the grandfather of coaching and the inspiration for my work. And the late Abraham Maslow, whose early work on emotional needs and values laid the foundation for this book.

Sandy Vilas, the owner of CoachInc.com, for your ongoing support and encouragement. I appreciate everything you have done and continue to do for me and the coaching community.

Thom Politico, my first-ever coach. I am ever grateful to you for getting me on the right career path years ago.

My amazing and inspiring clients Melissa Todd, Quinn Simpson, and Ali Brown for your willingness to share your hopes, dreams, fears, and successes in this book so that others can be inspired by your brilliant examples. Thank you for your candor, courage, and leadership in the world. And a heartfelt thank-you to all my clients whose stories bring this book to life. I am grateful to have had the opportunity to impact your lives and hope that your stories inspire others to find the careers and lives of their dreams.

Ronnie Slavis, amazing soul storyteller, for reminding me to play and have some fun! Thank you for your generous gift and fascinating story.

My dearest friends, Kate, Dave, Tracey, John, Allegra, Erik, Sam, Tony, Sally, Rachel, Debbi, and Colin, for always being there for me even when I fail to keep up with correspondence and calls. I love you all from the bottom of my heart and treasure our time together. Kate, an extra special thanks to you for being my writing buddy on this book. I'm looking forward to seeing your own book in print next!

All my readers and fans who have sent me countless e-mails and letters about your own success stories. It inspires me to keep on writing when I know my books are being read and make a real difference in your lives.

The Manitowoc Public Library and all its tremendously helpful and friendly staff.

And above all, my wonderful husband, Paul, for your love, support, and sense of humor even when I zone out completely and don't even hear a word that you say as I hammer away at the keyboard. I love you with all my heart.

Introduction

Are you trapped in a job you hate, but can't let it go because you are afraid it is the best you can find? Maybe your job is just OK, and you don't feel as if you've tapped into your full potential. Or your work doesn't allow you to live your dreams. Perhaps you fantasize about quitting your job and starting your own business, but you can't make the leap or don't know where to start. Are you treading water until things change, or until the economy improves? Or you have been a stay-at-home mother or father and now want to go back to work, but you don't know how to get started or what options are available to you to give you the time you need at home? Have you been downsized and unable to find a job in your industry? Perhaps you are waiting for retirement to start really enjoying your life. Whether you are a recent graduate wondering what sort of career you should pursue, whether you've been laid off, whether you are sick and tired of your current career and looking for something more fulfilling, or whether you are about to retire and are looking for something fun and engaging to keep your brain and body invigorated, this book is for you. In it, I've created a simple, seven-step program for finding and attracting your ideal career.

Wherever you are, you are in good company. Even with unemployment rates higher than ever, more than 50 percent of the population say they are in a job that they don't like. If you don't enjoy your work or are unemployed, this may have a negative effect on the rest of your life. It is hard to spend eight or more hours a day doing something you don't enjoy and then feel good about yourself, your life, and your relationships. Now is the time to make a change. There is no point wasting your life doing something you don't like when there are so many opportunities around us. Thanks to technology and the Internet, more than at any other point in the history of humanity, you now have the ability to design and create work that is perfectly suited to your natural talents, your personality, your inherent abilities, and your interests and passions. Whether that pays well is another question, but we'll get to that! The perfect combination is to find out your unique talents and abilities, what your passions and interests are, and how to combine those in a career that provides the money you need.

Rather than work hard and struggle to find the career you desire, I'd recommend a different, somewhat counterintuitive approach—attract the perfect job to you. There are two primary ways to get what we want in life: (1) set a goal, create a strategy and action plan, and go for it; or (2) attract it to you effortlessly. In this current economic climate, jobs are scarce—this is true. Nevertheless, if you complete the simple exercises in this book, you'll dramatically increase your chances of finding or creating the perfect job for you. In this book, I'll cover the essential elements that make up an ideal career so that you can crystallize your ideal job description. Knowing exactly what you want makes it much easier to find the right opportunity. Then I'll give you some practical ways to transition into the career or business you really want.

There a few basic questions you will need to answer in order to identify and find the ideal career:

1. What do I need? (personally and emotionally)
2. What do I want? (dreams, goals, desires, ideal life/career)
3. What am I good at? (skills, natural abilities and talents, personal style)
4. What do I enjoy? (passions, interests, values)
5. Where am I in my life? What's right for me now? (just out of school, midlife career change, retiring, reentering the workplace)
6. What people do I know? (contacts, friends, network, connections)
7. How do I make the transition? (reserves of time and money, networking and making contacts, making the right impression, etc.)

The simple exercises and assignments in this seven-step program will help you answer the preceding questions so that you can clearly articulate and define exactly what you want to do. This achievement will make it much easier for you to attract the best business and professional opportunities to you. I'll never forget when I was taking a personal development course and met a man who ran his own extremely successful consulting firm in Connecticut. I thought it would be an amazing place to work. When he asked me what I wanted to do and what I was good at, my jaw dropped open, and I had no idea what to say. I only knew what I didn't like—my banking job—and couldn't articulate what I really wanted. I muttered something vague about being a people person and wanting to work with people. The truth was I didn't know what I wanted to do, and I was twenty-nine years old. I've met clients who are fifty-five and say the same thing. I blew my chance of working for this company by blowing my very first impression.

After reading this book, you'll be fully prepared to say exactly what you want in a career and to go for what you want directly without wasting time pursuing jobs or careers you'll only want to leave soon after starting. If you can't clearly articulate in one to three sentences your ideal career, if you don't know what it is that you value most or what your natural talents are, then read on and you'll soon find out!

The first step is about window washing. We'll do a little housekeeping, both literally and figuratively. Often people can't see what their vision in life is if their windows are dirty. Scrub the dirt off and suddenly everything becomes so much clearer. I've included a checklist program that you can use to see if there are any areas in your life that need a bit of attention. And yes, I'm not kidding: you may need to actually wash your windows! It often helps when we are looking for a new career to work on areas that we can control immediately, such as clearing out the clutter in the office and home; that makes it easier to figure out what you really want. It is important to eliminate all the unnecessary distractions first. Otherwise, it can be difficult to achieve the clarity you seek.

Part of this necessitates that you identify your personal requirements. This approach may not be what you'd expect in a career book, but if you don't know what you need both personally and professionally, you may end up pursuing the wrong career path and wasting thousands of dollars and years of time unnecessarily. One of my clients had gone to engineering school and became an engineer—even though she hated it—so that she could gain her father's approval. If you don't know what your personal needs are, you may make the same mistake and take on educational programs or even careers in the attempt to fulfill your own unmet needs. You may think this is silly, but our personal requirements are powerful and will drive us to do all sorts of things, even getting a law degree you don't really want or becoming an engineer when you are really a people person. There are much easier ways to get your requirements satisfied.

I've made it really easy for you to identify your own top four personal requirements with a simple quiz you can take in about twenty minutes. Not only will this exercise help prevent you from making the wrong career and business choices, but also, getting your needs fulfilled will have the bonus side effect of making you much more attractive to potential employers or clients. We all know that neediness is unattractive, but we may not know what our own top four personal requirements are. Well worth the twenty minutes!

Once you've identified your personal requirements, we'll look at what your dreams and goals are. What would be an ideal life and career for you? It isn't any good to take on a career only to discover that it conflicts with your ideal life.

The next step is to identify your natural talents, strengths, and abilities with some simple and fun assignments. The secret to being effortlessly successful is to know what your natural and unique talents and abilities are. It makes sense that if you are hardwired to do something really well, with a little bit of training and practice you'll become masterful at this task or job. Most people find that doing something that they are good at is also personally rewarding and fulfilling. This is one of the easiest ways to find work that not only pays well but also gives you that feeling of fulfillment and enjoyment. Yes, you got that right: work does not have to be a struggle. In fact, if you are struggling, that is a sure sign that you haven't discovered your natural talents or abilities.

Then we'll take a look at your passions, interests, and values—the things that you really love to do in life, the stuff that would have you gleefully jumping out of bed in the morning to do. You can retire the snooze alarm and those umpteen cups of coffee you used to need to jump-start your day, because when you do something you are passionate about, you will be naturally motivated and can wean yourself off the artificial stimulants you've been using to get through the day.

Then we'll look at where you are in life. If you are a recent graduate, working eighty hours a week might sound like fun, whereas if you are sixty-five and hoping to slow down a bit, that won't sound at all appealing. You'll work on creating a life plan and career profile that will help you define the right career or business at this time.

Finally, we'll explore how you actually make that transition to your new career or business. What are the means to finding that dream job you've now defined? How do you pay the mortgage and start your own business? How do you manage your fears? What are the practical steps to making your ideal career a reality? How do you network your way to a new career? And as a bonus, after Step 7 I've included a chapter with some extra tips that seem to work like magic to speed up the whole career-change process.

As you read along, you'll see there are extended personal accounts at the end of some chapters in a section called "Success Story." This is where I share the nitty-gritty on how some of my coaching clients have worked through this program to find or create their new careers or businesses. Learn how actual clients have used these seven steps to transition into an ideal career or start a business. This feature concludes with me interviewing these clients; some have given me permission to use their real names. Feel free to check out their websites or go to my website at Lifecoach .com to read about additional client success stories. Many people hire me when they feel frustrated and stuck in a career that isn't fulfilling or satisfying even though it might have been very lucrative. The clients who have openly shared their stories are great examples of how very different people at various stages of their lives and careers can use the same seven-step program to create unique and personally rewarding new careers. Each of these clients has built a career or business around her ideal life and has chosen a path that honors her core values and passions. In some cases you'll notice that they value money and have been highly successful in creating profitable businesses or careers. And all of them are now making a bigger contribution to helping the world and others because they are doing what they have a natural talent and passion for. Yes, you can do this too!

Remember that life is a grand experiment! I hope you are sufficiently motivated by the real-life examples of people—who have successfully made the transition from doing work they didn't enjoy to creating the careers of their dreams—to take the time to do the practical exercises. It doesn't matter whether you are just starting out or are a senior executive on a solid career path, because the steps to making the transition are essentially the same. The path to success is to start, however small or insignificant that first step may seem, and keep experimenting until you get it just right. Let's get going!

Perfect the Present

If you're not playing a big enough game, you'll screw up the game you're playing just to give yourself something to do.

—ANONYMOUS

If you aren't happy in your current job, you may be letting things slip a bit whether you are aware of it or not. The temptation to do this is perfectly understandable and natural. You may not even realize how much you've let slide. Perhaps you are less than ecstatic when you arrive at the office or are even downright cranky. Maybe you are showing up late on occasion, are calling in sick more often, or aren't paying as much attention to your wardrobe or appearance. You may be letting paperwork pile up or allowing your e-mail in-box to become clogged with messages. You may not be returning phone calls as promptly as you know you should. This is all pretty normal. It is hard to do our best when we aren't doing work that we enjoy. In a way, you are subtly or—in some cases—not so subtly sabotaging your career. You just can't be bothered, and it is probably starting to show. This situation can have a downward spiraling effect, not just on your career but on your personal life as well. If you come home exhausted and grouchy, your partner and friends may have a hard time cheering you up. They may eventually tire of your complaints and end the relationship or distance themselves from you when you need their support the most. If you continue to do work and do it badly, then you end up either getting stuck in the same job or getting fired. Now, being fired may be exactly what you wanted at some level, but it may not be the best way of finding the work you love.

> *It's no good running a pig farm badly for thirty years while saying, "Really I was meant to be a ballet dancer." By that time, pigs will be your style.*
>
> —QUENTIN CRISP

If you are single, you may not be too worried about getting the pink slip, but if you are supporting a family, being in this situation could present a serious financial problem. Best to avoid getting fired, as it is always easier to attract a new career when you already have one, even if it isn't a job you want to keep. A job is often better than no job. Prospective employers can't help but wonder why you don't have a job; if you are employed, then they are reassured that you are employable by somebody. If you are already unemployed, don't panic. In fact, there are so many unemployed people out there right now that you'll fit right in. There are plenty of ways to remain attractive to prospective employers. We'll cover that later on, but whatever you are doing, start by perfecting the present situation—whatever that may be. It is the fastest way to attract better people and opportunities.

Clear the Clutter

One of the easiest ways to make room for new opportunities is to get rid of all the old stuff that no longer applies. Clean out your desk so that when the new job arrives, you'll be ready to go. Toss out old files; pack up papers and important documents and send them to the company archives if they need storage. Remove any personal belongings that are in your desk. Clean up your in-box and e-mails. Leave your desk spotless every night. This sends a signal to your boss that you are on top of your work and ready for more responsibility.

> *My philosophy is that not only are you responsible for your life, but also doing the best at this moment puts you in the best place for the next moment.*
>
> —OPRAH WINFREY

In fact, clearing out clutter is such a great way to attract new and better opportunities into your life, go ahead and clear out the clutter at home too. Some of my clients find that they start attracting prime opportunities as soon as they clear out some of the junk in their lives. So, while it may not look as if you are working on getting a new job when you spend the weekend clearing out the garage, it is actually one of the most powerful moves you can make.

I'm rather attached to my clutter, having descended from a long line of die-hard pack rats. (Just in case you don't know, actual pack rats are rodents that live in the desert; they collect all the junk and trash they can find and make their dens out of it—their nests look like a pile of garbage!) There are a few quick cures for the human pack rats out there. First, most people ask the wrong question when they are evaluating whether to keep a thing or toss it. They ask themselves, "Could this be useful someday?" The problem with that question is that the answer is always going to be yes. You may not know how it could be useful, but it just may be. Instead of trashing the item in question, you shuffle it around. A much more effective question is, "Have I used this in the last six months?" If not, and it isn't a holiday ornament or a pair of winter skis, then out it goes. If it is a decorative object such as a painting, then you can ask, "Does this give me joy just by looking at it?" If it doesn't give you joy, then out it goes. These two questions will help average pack rats safely eliminate about 50 percent of their stuff. If you are still struggling to part with things and worry that you may need them, box them up, put today's date on the box, and stow it in a basement or garage. Mark your calendar six months forward as donation day. In six months' time, take the box straight to the charity shop. Do *not*—I repeat, do *not*—be tempted to open up the box. If you've safely managed for six months without the stuff, you don't need it now. If you open the top, you'll start pulling things out again and cluttering up your life.

Another very helpful tip is to put a numerical limit on things or to have only two extras. For example, you have twenty pairs of shoes, and that is your limit. If you buy a new pair of shoes, one of the old pairs has to go. It is easier to get rid of an old thing if your policy when buying something new is to ask, "Is this an upgrade?" If it isn't, then why are you buying it? For linens and towels, you can apply the two-extras rule. I have a set of linens for each bed and two extras. You can swiftly clear out the extraneous linens by choosing your three favorites. Obviously, get rid of, repair, or recycle anything that is torn, damaged, stained, or worn out.

According to the principles of feng shui, the ancient art of arranging your home and office so that it is most beneficial to you, all clutter represents stuck energy. Any clutter anywhere in your life is clogging up the flow. Get rid of clutter both at home and at work and I guarantee you that new things will come your way—perhaps a new job prospect or business opportunity will come knocking at your door.

Anytime I want some new clients, all I have to do is start cleaning out my files and deleting old e-mails and, bingo, a prospect calls or e-mails. I know it sounds like hocus-pocus, but it works. Nature abhors a vacuum, so if you create a vacuum (lots of empty space), you'll be much more attractive to new things, people, and opportunities. If you are stuck in a rut, start clearing the junk out of your life and things will soon start to shift for you. A little tip: if you are more pack rat than minimalist by nature, I'd highly recommend getting in a friend or a professional organizer to help—it will go much faster and won't be nearly so painful.

Master Every Aspect of Your Work

The key to attracting a better opportunity is to first perfect your current job. This means that you should do your job 100 percent.

> *I don't want the cheese; I just want to get out of the trap.*
>
> —SPANISH PROVERB

Ironic though it is, the fastest way out of your current job is to completely master it. If you can't figure out why you are stuck in a rut at work, there may be some aspect of the job you have not mastered yet. Do you have an issue with a colleague or boss? Perhaps you are in this job to learn how to deal with a micromanaging boss, a toxic colleague, or corporate politics. *If* you don't master this challenge, then even if you get another job, you'll soon discover that you have the same issues—the micromanaging boss just has a different name now. On the other hand, once you've mastered the job issue you've been trying to hide from or deny, you will soon attract the next opportunity. This usually happens very quickly. Sometimes my clients just take this first step (perfect the present) and promptly get promoted within the company—the boss sees the renewed commitment and energy and doesn't realize it is energy to leave the company, and the person gets promoted or gets more interesting responsibilities—or they attract the interest of a competitor or are hired by a client.

When I was working at Chase, one of the business account representatives did his job so enthusiastically and so well that one of his customers hired him away, enticing him with a much larger salary! If he had been dragging his feet or complaining about his job, he wouldn't have attracted the interest of his new employer. The source of your next opportunity could very well be one of your current clients or customers. Or you may discover that you now like your job, once it's perfect, and decide to stick with it.

More often than not, when coaching clients come to me with a list of goals to accomplish for the year, they don't choose the goals that would make the biggest difference to the quality of their lives. We have a tendency to choose the wrong goals—the goals that we think we *should* have instead of the ones that we truly need or want. For example, you may think your life would be perfect if you had a fabulous career, but the place to really go to work may very well be on your energy and vitality. The optimal course isn't always obvious, so take the time to complete the simple quiz that follows and discover where to focus to get on the right path to your new career or job prospects.

Perfect the Present Quiz

Instructions: For each of the following statements, enter a *T* if it is true for you or an *F* if it is false. Add up your total True points at the end of each category.

ENERGY AND VITALITY

_____ I get all the sleep I need. I am not tired.
_____ I eat healthful, fresh foods and vegetables every day.
_____ My cholesterol count is within the desired range.

_____   I drink filtered or purified water throughout the day. I am
           well hydrated.

_____   I exercise three times a week or more.

_____   I have eliminated all sources of stress.

_____   I have something to look forward to each day.

_____   Nothing in my life is draining me.

_____   I take at least four holidays a year.

_____   I follow a nutritional plan designed for my body.

Total True = _____ (10 max)

TIME AND SPACE

_____   I am ten minutes early for business and personal
           appointments.

_____   I have an assistant who handles the personal and business
           things I'd prefer not to deal with.

_____   I always underpromise and overdeliver. For example, if I
           think I can get it done in one week, I tell the boss I'll have it
           done in two weeks. Then I turn it in early.

_____   I take at least ten minutes of every day to sit and do
           nothing or meditate.

_____   I can easily say no and have learned to decline gracefully.

_____   I take evenings and weekends off consistently.

_____   I keep one to two hours unscheduled every day.

_____   I have a life plan. I don't have to get everything done this
           year.

_____   I pay my bills online or automatically.

_____   I order my groceries online and have them delivered
           weekly.

Total True = _____ (10 max)

LOVE AND RELATIONSHIPS

_____   I treat everyone with great respect.

_____   I know five very successful people and can call on them for
           advice and support.

_____ My personal and emotional needs are fully satisfied. (Take the free Emotional Index Quiz at Lifecoach.com if you aren't sure what your needs are.)

_____ I have ended relationships that drain my energy or damage me.

_____ I have fully forgiven those people who have hurt or damaged me, whether their actions were intentional or not.

_____ I have apologized and/or made amends to anyone I might have hurt or damaged, whether my actions were intentional or not.

_____ I am happy with the amount of time I spend with my family/children/friends.

_____ I have a best friend or soul mate.

_____ No one in my life is trying to change me.

_____ I receive enough love from people around me to feel great.

Total True = _____ (10 max)

MONEY AND FINANCES

_____ I currently save at least 10 percent of my income.

_____ I always pay my bills on time or early.

_____ I am putting aside enough money each month to reach financial independence.

_____ My income is stable and predictable.

_____ I currently live well within my means and do not overspend.

_____ I have returned any money I have borrowed.

_____ I have six months' living expenses in a money-market-type savings account.

_____ I am on a career or business path that is or will soon be financially and personally rewarding.

_____ I have no credit card or unsecured debts.

_____ My will or trust is up to date and accurate.

Total True = _____ (10 max)

HOME AND COMFORT

_____ My home is clean and comfortable.

_____ I like every room in my home.

_____ I have a special place to relax or curl up.

_____ I have extra room (for new things, guests, etc.).

_____ My bed is made every day.

_____ I have nothing around the home or in storage that I do not need or enjoy.

_____ I live in the geographic area of my choice.

_____ My bedroom lets me have the best sleep possible (mattress, light, air).

_____ I live in a home that I love.

_____ I am not tolerating anything about my home.

Total True = _____ (10 max)

SELF-CARE AND HEALTH

_____ I have a weekly massage or bodywork.

_____ My weight is in the healthy range.

_____ I like my body just the way it is.

_____ My hair and nails look great.

_____ I sleep on sheets with a thread count of three hundred or better.

_____ I meditate or write in a journal daily.

_____ I have no unhealthful habits or addictions (caffeine, alcohol, sugar, TV, cigarettes).

_____ I engage in daily exercise that gives me joy.

_____ I wear quality sunglasses to protect my eyes.

_____ I get sunshine or take the appropriate vitamin D (cod-liver oil) supplements daily.

Total True = _____ (10 max)

CAREER AND OPPORTUNITY

_____ I know my strengths and natural abilities and delegate my weaknesses.

_____ I have work, a career, or a business that is financially and personally rewarding.

_____ I have a mentor and/or coach who supports me in reaching my objectives.

_____ I get along well with my colleagues and managers.

_____ I have mastered my craft/skill/job.

_____ I have a strong network of successful people whom I can count on for help if I need it.

_____ I continually invest 10 percent in mastering and developing my skills and strengths.

_____ I attract success; I don't strive for it or chase it.

_____ I have all the equipment and tools to do my work well (ergonomic keyboard, chair, etc.).

_____ I surround myself with inspiring and supportive people.

Total True = _____ (10 max)

ATTRACTION

_____ I effortlessly attract the best people and opportunities. I do not have to sell myself or seduce others.

_____ I don't just listen to people; I really hear and understand them.

_____ I communicate fully in the moment. I am not afraid to speak my mind.

_____ I am grateful for the people in my life, and they feel this appreciation.

_____ I put people first, results second.

_____ I put my personal and emotional needs first.

_____ I have bigger boundaries than I need.

_____ I give the gifts that others really want.

_____ It is natural and effortless for me to be generous with my time, money, and attention.

_____ I may want a tremendous amount, but I don't have to have it. I am free.

Total True = _____ (10 max)

HAPPINESS AND JOY

_____   I start and end each day with a routine that nurtures me and gives me joy.

_____   My work is personally rewarding and fulfilling. I look forward to doing my work virtually every day.

_____   I take pleasure and delight in the little things (a perfect cup of tea, the sunset, the first snowdrop, a bubble bath).

_____   I know my strengths and do not waste time trying to master my weaknesses. I know that my strengths are enough. I don't have to be good at everything.

_____   I have delegated, automated, or systematized all tasks that I find unpleasant or disagreeable (cleaning, cooking, taxes, etc.).

_____   There is nothing I am dreading or avoiding. I am complete with all unresolved issues from the past.

_____   I am beyond striving for success; I simply enjoy my life and focus on what fulfills me.

_____   I use the joy filter for decision making: I say no to the things I don't enjoy or want in my life.

_____   I have a close circle of friends and family that I love and enjoy.

_____   I know what makes me happy, and I do those activities consistently.

Total True = _____ (10 max)

Compare your total True points for each of the nine sections. Where you score the lowest may be the area that needs your attention the most.

Answer Key

ENERGY AND VITALITY

0–5 pts.   Your level of energy and vitality is low. There is no reason why you should tolerate this deficiency. Your life will be easier if you focus on this area. Give yourself permission to eliminate all the sources of stress in your life, and start taking better care of yourself. Look at what activities you can eliminate, postpone, or delegate. Ask for help from friends and family, or hire help if you need to. Hide the TV in a closet and get to bed earlier so you can get up earlier and meditate, walk, and get some exercise.

6–10 pts.   Keep up the good work! The more energy you have, the easier it is to accomplish all that you want to do.

TIME AND SPACE

0–5 pts.   You are running around like a headless chicken. You may be addicted to the adrenaline rush of running late, showing up just on time, or doing too much. Start by simply showing up ten minutes early to every appointment and you will begin to create the feeling of having more than enough time in your life. If you are too busy and stressed, you'll miss out on opportunities. Try cutting out caffeine as well to get off the adrenaline addiction. Learn to say no, and say it often.

6–10 pts.   Well done! Continue to carve out time for yourself and you'll attract even better opportunities. Creativity needs time and space. As you give yourself more than enough time, you'll be able to access your innate creativity.

LOVE AND RELATIONSHIPS

0–5 pts.   You may not realize that your unfulfilled personal and emotional needs are driving away the love and people you most want to attract. This situation is completely curable. Take the Personal Requirements Quiz in Step 2 or the online version at Lifecoach.com, and identify your top four personal needs. Then take action to satisfy them in healthful and appropriate ways. For suggestions on how to do this, please see the Resources section in the back. If you are even the tiniest bit "needy," you'll end up repelling people and opportunities. Get your needs fulfilled and you'll start attracting them instead!

6–10 pts. Good! You maintain strong boundaries and have surrounded yourself with people who love and care about you. You do not associate with negative people and have forgiven those who have hurt you.

MONEY AND FINANCES

0–5 pts. You are struggling financially, and this is no way to live. It is impossible to be your best if you are living with financial stress. This condition is fixable. Downsize; cut your expenses by 50 percent until you are earning more than enough to pay the bills. Financial stress can damage your health and your relationships—it isn't worth it. Do what you need to do to get yourself on solid footing. If you are burdened by debt, consult a nonprofit credit-counseling service for assistance. Start saving 10 percent of your income even if you have debts. Track your expenses down to the penny in a daily written log. Cut out all extraneous and unnecessary expenses immediately. You can get out of debt and turn your financial life around. See the Resources section or go to Lifecoach.com for more information.

6–10 pts. You are on the right path. Now you may want to get on the path to financial independence so that you have enough money or income streams that you don't have to work for a living. Find more tips in my first book, *Coach Yourself to Success*.

HOME AND COMFORT

0–5 pts. Instead of nurturing you, your home is another source of stress. Do what it takes to have a clean and tidy residence, even if that means hiring a house cleaner to come and help. If you are a single parent, you need more help in the house than you realize. Even if you hire a cleaner to come only once a month to help with the big clean, that is a step in the right direction. Take the time to make your home a haven where you can relax upon entering.

6–10 pts.   Good work! Your home is a comfortable, relaxing place to recharge. The more points you get, the more energy you will get just by being in your home. Now is the time to perfect one room at a time until you love every single one of them.

SELF-CARE AND HEALTH

0–5 pts.   You simply aren't investing enough in your self-care and health. You have only one body to last a lifetime, so make health a number one priority. Without our health, we cannot enjoy our relationships, our work, or our lives. If you can't get motivated to start, hire a personal trainer to create a program for you at the gym. Or work with a nutritionist for the ideal food plan and you'll be on the way.

6–10 pts.   You might have already noticed that the better you take care of yourself, the better others will take care of you too! Now is the time to take your self-care up to the next level. Add in that extra treatment or massage.

CAREER AND OPPORTUNITY

0–5 pts.   There is no reason why you should dread going to work each day. Most people can find work that is personally fulfilling and financially rewarding. It is worth doing a bit of navel-gazing and discovering what your natural abilities are and what career options are best suited to your natural style and personality. You've certainly picked up the right book! You'll find more information and helpful computerized assessment programs in the Resources section at the back or on Lifecoach.com.

6–10 pts.   You are on the path to a rewarding career. Congratulations! Continue to invest in your ongoing development and growth so that you don't become obsolete, which can happen quickly in today's rapidly changing world. Leverage your strengths, and give up on getting good at your weaknesses—delegate them responsibly instead. You will gain more by focusing on and mastering your natural strengths than you ever will by working on your weaknesses.

ATTRACTION

0–5 pts.   You are working much harder than need be to achieve the success you want. Life doesn't have to be so difficult. Stop struggling, and start attracting the people, love, and opportunities you most desire. Attracting what you want starts with identifying your unfulfilled personal requirements. Once you get this aspect sorted out, you'll be amazed at how much easier life becomes. You will attract better people and opportunities in your personal and professional lives.

6–10 pts.   Congratulations! You have stopped struggling and are naturally attracting the people and opportunities you want. The key to staying in this effortless flow is having gratitude for the people around you. Say thanks at least five times a day with a note or phone call.

HAPPINESS AND JOY

0–5 pts.   You may be too busy and might have lost touch with the simple things that give you pleasure and joy. Start by adding ten daily pleasures to your life (a hot bubble bath, a picnic lunch in the local park, a brisk walk with the dog). Consider what activities make you happy. If you aren't doing them on a regular basis, it is no surprise that happiness eludes you.

6–10 pts.   Well done! You have slowed down enough to savor the richness and joy of daily life. You are wise enough to know that it is a joy to be sad when you are sad and it is a joy to be angry when you are angry. The present is always perfect even when it isn't.

Congratulations! Now that you've completed the Perfect the Present Quiz, you've probably discovered a few areas that need attention. Ideally, aim to get 1–3 new points on this quiz each week. Don't worry, you can do this while working on the steps outlined to reinvent your career as well.

Handle Any Problems with Your Manager and Colleagues

The next part of perfecting your present situation is addressing problems and issues with your current manager or colleagues. This is an extremely important part of finding the perfect career. Sometimes my clients want to quit a job because they don't like their particular boss or colleagues. If this is the case for you, then I've got bad news: if you don't learn to manage the situation you are currently in, you are likely to end up in the exact same situation at your new job. Life is a demanding instructor, and if you don't learn how to handle something, you don't get to pass Go and collect your $200. You may have a new boss or new job, but all too soon the same old issues and problems will crop up again. More bad news: it's you, not them. Let's suppose for example that your boss micromanages you, and you can't stand it, so you resist. This resistance usually shows up in the workplace as passive-aggressive behavior. You don't tell your boss that you won't do that report, but then you turn it in a day or two late. This tactic isn't going to win you any brownie points.

> *Everything that irritates us about others can lead us to an understanding of ourselves.*
>
> —CARL JUNG

Let's try a more productive strategy. Make a list of all the people at work with whom you have issues or problems right now (micromanaging or controlling boss, manager who takes all the credit, back-stabbing colleague, etc.):

NAME	PROBLEM
1. _____	_____
2. _____	_____
3. _____	_____

4. _____   _____

5. _____   _____

Good. Now let's see if we can find some cures for these fairly common problems. If your boss micromanages you, then you need to set up some boundaries. Let your boss know that you do your best work if you are given free rein. Ask how much feedback your boss wants (most micromanaging bosses have the need to be in control). Make sure you meet his or her need. Even better, go overboard. One client had a new and highly controlling manager. She resented the fact that her boss wanted her to compile a weekly report outlining all the activities for the week in a summary. She felt it was a waste of time, so she often delayed doing it until she was asked where the report was. This behavior wasn't endearing her to the boss, who then trusted her even less. The employee took charge of the situation and did a complete 180-degree turnaround. She started writing lengthy reports full of details and turning them in on time each week and then calling her manager so that they could pore over the contents together. After a few weeks of this, the manager started to relax and told her she had to do the report only once a month and it needed to be only one page long. Victory!

This example demonstrates that if you satisfy your boss's personal requirements, however idiosyncratic they may be, then you'll find they disappear or diminish. The boss who feels in control will come across as less controlling. On the other hand, if that requirement isn't being met, then your boss will try all the harder to control you. If you rebel and deprive your superiors of what they need, you'll only exacerbate the situation and make your own work life miserable. So, not only will knowing what your own personal requirements are benefit your career, but also it really helps to know what your boss needs if you want to get that plum job or promotion. Read the next chapter to pinpoint what your personal requirements are and how to satisfy them in a professional manner. If you know what your own personal and emotional requirements are, it is easier to identify and satisfy your manager's requirements, and you'll both be happier as a result.

The vast majority of problems with people can be solved with these two steps: (1) put in place stronger boundaries, and (2) get your own personal and emotional requirements met at home, *not* at work. Sounds simple and ridiculously obvious, and it is, but it isn't easy to do, so most people don't do it. In fact, since most people don't even know what their personal requirements are, you'll be way ahead of the game by figuring out your own. This knowledge will give you a huge advantage in the workplace, and it will automatically improve your professional and networking ability as well. I'll explain how to do both in Step 2.

SUCCESS STORY

The Frustrated Human Resources Director Who Followed Her Passion to Find the Right Path

Melissa Todd, a vivacious, stunning, redheaded, forty-something HR director, was making an impressive six-figure salary at a law firm in Washington, D.C., but hadn't been loving her job for years. It didn't take much work on identifying her passions and values (Step 5) to figure out that Melissa is a bona fide dog lover—the kind of person who creates an immediate bond with any dog that she meets—and to no surprise, dogs love her too! That's nice, but how do you make money out of a love of dogs? Of course, she had two dogs of her own, but she couldn't see how loving dogs could make her a good living.

One of her first coaching assignments was to start a business in the evenings doing something she enjoyed. Melissa's first business venture was to create special dog packages complete with beds, handmade collars, hand-painted feeding bowls, special treats, and toys, geared for celebrity pets staying in luxury hotels. The problem with this business was that profit margins just weren't enough to make it a sustainable or lucrative career, and although the products were for dogs, it didn't fulfill her desire for actual contact with the animals. She thought of volunteering at dog shelters in her spare time, but that wasn't a moneymaking proposition either, and she was too tempted to adopt the dogs herself.

Melissa then came up with the idea of running her own dog day-care business in Austin, Texas. She calls it Hip Hounds. Again, Melissa knew that she required financial security, so she started the business while still working full-time at the law firm. She used her evenings and weekends to take out a business loan, research the best location for a dog day-care center in Austin, buy a desirable facility, and hire the managers and staff to run it while she carried on with her work at the firm.

Needless to say, she didn't have much spare time on her hands, but keeping her day job gave her the financial security she felt she needed to know she didn't have to make an immediate or huge profit from her business. She knew she had the income to pay her home mortgage and other obligations. Far better to be busy than financially stressed! Working full-time also forced her to define the procedures and policies in a manual and train and hire a full-time manager and staff to operate the place without her. This freed her up to work on the more interesting projects such as marketing campaigns to get new clients (dogs) for her venture.

Talane interviews her client, Melissa:

What was your career like before you started Hip Hounds?

Being HR director of a large law firm required working with a lot of stressed-out, busy people. That, in and of itself, was a career change. I was an attorney before that and wasn't happy with that, so I went on to become an HR director at the law firm, thinking it would be more fulfilling. But had I had coaching earlier, I would have realized that people were not my passion; dogs were!

How did doing the work on identifying and satisfying your personal requirements and needs make a difference?

It is so important to realize what it is in life that you actually crave. For me, that was security and balance. I knew that financial security was a need of mine, but I had no idea about the balance thing.

And boy, did I have an unbalanced life—constant travel, stress, not sleeping. I was totally in the wrong field for someone who needed balance. My corporate existence was always up and down. I was moving to places where I didn't particularly want to live for a job that I didn't particularly enjoy. It was total unbalance. Balance seemed so foreign—so boring to me. I want to be going, going, going all the time, so why would I need balance? Now I see that I can't be myself without it and that it was impossible for me to achieve balance while working at the law firm. How can you be balanced if you wake up in the middle of the night worrying about some personnel issue?

Doing the values work confirmed that one of my values is to contribute. It became glaringly obvious that my values were not in alignment with the law firm's. I remember a time toward the end of my career at the law firm: I was disenchanted with the budget meetings, how many new clients, the money—the business was all focused on money. I have a strong sense of right and wrong and a need for justice, which is one reason why I became a prosecutor in the first place. I got thoroughly disgusted when our firm decided to represent a client who was charged with dog abuse, which I was disgusted by.

I expressed my disagreement with that decision to the partners. I suggested they survey the employees and ask them how many were dog lovers before they committed. The fact that I had worked there and was a director for seven years made no difference. No one wanted to even discuss the matter. It was all about the bottom line. The managing partner totally ignored it. It goes against my core values. I thought everyone there was better than that. Employees were so upset that we'd associate the company name with this client's name. This isn't me. This is not what I wanted to associate myself with. We are a civil law firm. Why are we doing this for the money? Valuewise, I was very upset. Things were prerecession and slowing down, so they saw the PR and money as a good thing. That was the final straw for me. It became very clear to me that my values were not going to be honored or respected working for this law firm. I resigned soon after that.

How did following your passions and values help you find the right career/ business?

I used to make beautiful, handmade dog collars to sell in a boutique—just something I did because I liked to do it. My best friend was the director of sales at the Ritz Carlton in New York, and she hooked me up with the other head in D.C. I had lunch with her, and we were talking about putting together a pet package for Billy Joel's dog—a cute little pug—a nice bed, personalized Ritz Carlton dog tag to wear while they were there, some special dog treats. We did dog packages for a few stars. So, I started putting together dog packages with hand-painted bowls and special beds and collars. I made a little money doing it, but I soon began to think that there had to be a way I could make enough money in a business to quit my legal job. Although it was fun to create these dog packages, the business just didn't have enough income potential. I realized that people need services, and there is more markup in that. Soon all the corporate hotels started doing their own stuff, so there wasn't that much business. It was fun to do it for celebrities, though. That was all part of my status phase. Now that isn't that important to me anymore. I goofed around with that business on evenings and weekends. I was seeing more doggie day cares in New York and in D.C. and thought, hey, I could do this. When I was in college, I used to volunteer at the dog centers. I always knew that dogs were my passion, but I suppressed it because I didn't think there was a viable business in it.

Thinking back on it, when I graduated from college, I had two job offers for tiny salaries doing work as a news reporter. My father was worried it wouldn't be enough money and encouraged me to go to law school because he thought journalism was a silly career. Funny enough, my dad didn't even finish college himself! He said he'd pay for me to go to law school if I got in, so I did. I was doing it for him, not for me. I had been on the right path. I was a journalism major, and I wanted to be a TV reporter. I'm still fascinated with CNN. If I could, I'd be a Diane Sawyer. My second fascination, after dogs, is news and current events. Who knows but that might be what is next for me now that Hip Hounds is running so smoothly.

But who works on these needs and values assessments until they are in their forties? Guidance and career counselors don't work through these exercises. All this time, I didn't know who I was or what was important to me. I knew I was missing something, but I couldn't put a finger on it until we did all that work on identifying my personal requirements and values. I never in a million years would have guessed I needed balance, for example. And spending time clearly defining my values was very important. Then I could see clearly what was missing in my work and what I needed to make me happy. Quite honestly, the Myers-Briggs stuff (a personality assessment) is interesting, but the values and needs exercises are far more important. They are much more valuable tools. Life is all about values and needs. You aren't going to be happy unless you meet those needs (take the Personal Requirements Quiz in Step 2) and are living those values. It's as simple as that.

Law school wasn't a total waste of time. I liked the criminal law and prosecution work—I saw it as a way to make a difference in people's lives, make a little money, and give back to society—but I wasn't passionate about the law. I didn't want to go to law school, but people said to go. So, I did. Now I'd advise students to really get clear on their values before they go to school and to follow their hearts. Otherwise, you will be on the wrong track and will waste years of your life trying to make someone else happy. It's your life, and you can't make someone else happy by being miserable!

We didn't use the envy exercise (described in Step 5), but is there someone out there that you envy?

If I looked at people I envy, it would be after reading an article about people who are doing dog rescue work or setting up foundations for dogs. The woman who started guide dogs for the blind—I'd love to be that woman. On the other hand, when I was in my twenties, I'd say I'd envy Diane Sawyer. You get to meet such interesting and fascinating people. Or Katie Couric. I loved the journalism. That is one of the things I'm passionate about and why I majored in journalism. I've always thought it would be wonderful to be one of those people who do the pet segments and bring dogs in there for adoption—being some kind of pet expert on TV. That is something I can still do: parlay my experience into media somehow. That may be the next thing.

What did you do for fun as a kid?

I used to write. I loved traveling so much. I kept a journal about everything we did on family vacations and wrote short stories when I was ten. I loved writing. That is why I went to journalism school, but then I got off track thanks to my well-meaning parents, who wanted the first lawyer in the family. We always had dogs when I was growing up, and one of my favorite memories from when I was two and three is playing with all the animals on my relative's farm. There are photos of me kissing the dogs on the tip of the nose, lots of pictures of me with animals. We had dogs, cats. As a child, it was all about dogs, farm animals, and writing—quite an interesting combination of bizarre things that make me unique!

What was the shift for you in finally quitting your day job?

After year one, Hip Hounds was starting to break even and was even turning a profit ahead of time. I had budgeted it to be profit- able by year two, so this was a pleasant surprise. I was steadily paying back the business loan, and my accountant was impressed with the prospects for the business. It was starting to look good, not just in concept but also on paper. Even then, I was terrified to let go of my day job. I held on to my day job until I realized that in the past six months of working I had saved only $5,000. You reminded me that the point of the day job was to provide financial security and that if I had spent those forty-plus hours a week for six months on marketing for new dogs, I would easily have made more than the $5,000. So, all of the sudden, the financial reasons for keeping the day job had disappeared, and it made sense to quit and work on Hip Hounds full-time. You gave me the coaching assignment of writing my letter of resignation—an assignment that was really easy to do! It was turning it in to my boss that was the hard part.

What was the turning point for you?

I just got to the point where I was so tired all the time. You told me something very important that really hit home: you said that time was something you can never get back, but money you can always make. I'm in my forties; I'm not getting any younger. I realized that I had to do this now because I won't have the energy in my fifties. I was ready. I had all my finances in order. Actually, I always had the money; it was just a matter of realizing that it was going to be OK. My worst-case scenario if things didn't work out as planned was to find another HR job or legal job. That was my safety net.

What is your career/life like now?

Now that I've created so much free time for myself, I'm ready for the next adventure. What am I going to do with my time other than giving back to the dog rescue group and working out every day at the gym? Time to pursue another passion. Hip Hounds is now running as smooth as a clock, and I've created a life with income coming in and free time to do what I want to do. It has all come true! Now I am afraid I'll get a little bored, so soon I'll need another project!

If you could do it differently now, what would you do?

You were always coaching me to save money and stop filling up my empty life with purchases—clothes, trips, drinks, whatever it was—to fill up that void because I was working in a job that wasn't making me happy. If I hadn't been spending all that money, I would have had my dream earlier. I needed to recognize I was spending all this money to compensate for a job that really sucked. Now I don't spend nearly as much as I used to. I used to think that if I couldn't shop at Nordstrom, then I wouldn't be happy. I don't care about a pair of Chanel sunglasses anymore. I still have a few good pieces, but now I love shopping at Target—I am just as happy with a cute T-shirt. I was caught up in the whole image/career thing where people are concerned about what you wear and what you drive. Now I don't need a BMW or a fancy suit or shoes. I just need a big vehicle to haul a lot of dogs around. One of the most liberating things I did was give all my suits to the charity Dress for Success (another one of your suggestions)—getting rid of all the trappings of my old career. Once I got rid of everything that didn't apply to my new life, I felt so free.

What do your friends and family say now?

Now that I've made it, my dad is really proud of me and of the business. He brought his friend over, whose son is a lawyer, to see my facility. But still to this day, I told him about my plans to take a one-month skiing sabbatical and he said, "I just don't understand how you can leave your business for a month." He just doesn't get it, but he is proud of me. I knew that when he brought his friend over to see the operation. My friends now tell me I was so grumpy when I worked at the law firm. Now they say I'm the way I'm supposed to be: happy, relaxed, fun-loving. When people see me with the dogs, they say, "Oh my God, that is what you were meant to do; you just glow when you are out there with them."

What advice do you have for others?

Do it sooner rather than later. I would repeat what you told me: time is the only thing you can't get back; you can always make more money. If you have a need for financial security, start your business on the side to give yourself the comfort level you need.

I wish, when you started talking to me about saving money and making a bigger nest egg, that I had started doing it sooner. I was in a place where I was still buying things to fill a void. Why do something that makes you miserable every day? My fear was financial even though it wasn't a real fear, because I had a lot of money in savings and I could have found another job. The needs and values are so important. Now I know clearly what I need (my personal requirements)—what my mind and body must have—and don't confuse that with wants.

For more information about Hip Hounds, please see Melissa's website at hiphounds.com.

Identify Your Personal Requirements

If the essential care of the person
is denied or suppressed, he
gets sick sometimes in obvious
ways, sometimes in subtle
ways, sometimes immediately,
sometimes later.

—ABRAHAM MASLOW

If you have been downsized or pink-slipped or just can't seem to find work these days, or if you keep getting overlooked for that promotion, the first thing to realize is that it probably isn't personal. It will feel very personal, but in most cases it isn't. The economy is changing; jobs that used to exist are now being eliminated, and new ones are opening up that you may not even be aware of. The pace of change is relentless and impersonal. It used to take one generation to replace a job with machines or technology, and now it takes only four to five years, and that number is rapidly decreasing. You know that if you buy a computer, it is already obsolete, and the plans for the newer, better, faster one are already in the works. The U.S. Department of Labor reports that 50 percent of the jobs that we will have in the next six years have not yet been created. The average length of a job in America is only 3.2 years. Do the math and you'll discover that the average person will have fourteen to sixteen jobs over the course of a forty-five-year work span. The days of working in one job for one company and getting that gold watch on retirement are long gone. Change is the name of the game today, which makes it all the more important to know what your inherent strengths and abilities are so that you can find the careers that best fit you.

One client had been given the pink slip and a year's worth of severance pay as well. She was angry and hurt about being fired. She spent the best part of her severance and wasted seven months fuming before she called me and started coaching. She had loved her work and couldn't believe that they would fire her. The first thing she had to understand was that it wasn't personal; it was political—but she just couldn't seem to get over it. Don't waste your own precious time. Get your personal and emotional needs met outside of work and you'll see that you suddenly project a cool demeanor of professional detachment. This is the secret to being detached from something you love. It will not only make you much more attractive to your current employer (assuming you have a job) but also make you more attractive to prospective employers. Get your personal requirements satisfied and you'll instantly be a more promising candidate.

Elizabeth, a fifty-something senior executive, hired me because her company had recently merged and she was now working with a new executive team. These folks weren't like her old team, and she didn't have much respect for them. They swore frequently, didn't listen, and didn't give her the respect she felt she deserved. She was passionate about her work but was so certain that she'd never get along with the managers that she hired me to help her find a new career. One of the assignments I gave her was to write down her ideal job description (you get to do that later!) and to work on getting her personal and emotional needs fulfilled at home, not at work.

So, Elizabeth took the Personal Requirements Quiz and discovered that her number one need was to be appreciated. She certainly wasn't getting much appreciation at work these days, so this state of affairs contributed to her frustration. I gave her an assignment to ask five people to meet her need to be appreciated at least once a week for the next eight weeks. She started with her sixteen-year-old daughter, who presented her a handmade card the first week telling her how much she loved her and appreciated her. She asked her closest friends to call once a week and leave a message regarding something they appreciated about the friendship. Her mother called weekly as well. Also, although she hadn't asked her husband (their relationship was on the rocks), he said he wanted to be part of her appreciation team and voluntarily wrote her a long letter citing all the things he appreciated and valued about her. Some of what he wrote took her by surprise. All this appreciation on the home front had an interesting effect at work: she no longer needed the appreciation in the office and was able to detach from her work emotionally—it was just a job now. This new detachment had an interesting effect as well: the new management team noticed her cool professionalism and liked it. In fact, the managers said they thought the coaching was really working and offered to reimburse her for it. They didn't know that she was actually trying to find new work altogether. Then, when a plum position opened up to be regional director in another state, they offered her the job! Elizabeth took it and loves it! So much for quitting.

If you are emotionally involved with your work, then you definitely need to take the Personal Requirements Quiz in this chapter or online at Lifecoach.com. If you are looking for a new job, then you must work on your personal requirements, because you may be coming across in interviews as desperate (unmet emotional needs always make us appear a bit needy, even if we don't realize it). Likewise, if you want to get promoted, get your needs met—if you don't need people, they are more likely to want you. We are always more confident and attractive when our needs are fulfilled. This is a critical element to finding the ideal career as well. You won't enjoy working for a controlling boss if one of your needs is independence or freedom. Or you could find yourself going to get an M.B.A. even though you really aren't a numbers person in order to get the approval of your parents. I had one client who became an engineer despite the fact that she hated every minute of it in order to get approval from her father, who was an engineer. Once she realized her true motivations, she was able to ask for her father's approval directly, quit her engineering job, and became a professional coach. She has never been happier. Once you have your needs fulfilled, you can do what you want, rather than trying to peg yourself into a career or life that you don't really want in order to get what you need.

One retired CEO in one of my phone classes commented, "I used to get up at four A.M. every day so that I was the first in the office, and I made a point of being the last one to leave as well. If I had only known that my need to be the best was driving me, I would have got a lot more sleep!" He also said that even though he had achieved the highest levels of career and financial success, and had a loving wife and children, underneath it all was this vague, rankling discontent. He was just never fully satisfied and couldn't figure out why, since he had done everything that he had thought would make him happy—until taking my phone class, when it all became incredibly clear. You can skip the needs part, but you'll do so at the risk of continually enduring this underlying dissatisfaction with life.

The central problem with our unmet needs is that they will drive us to engage in all sorts of negative behaviors—overeating, smoking, drinking, gambling, overspending—and we don't even know why we persist in doing it. In fact, you can consciously know you are doing something that you shouldn't be doing (as you stuff that second chocolate doughnut into your mouth) and yet feel compelled to do it anyway. Such is the power of our unmet needs. The reality is that most people can't even articulate what it is they need. Rather than try to tackle the addictive behavior, it is much more productive to tackle the hidden need that is driving it. More often than not, the behavior is then easy to stop. You can't get enough chocolate doughnuts if your real need is to be cherished. You can never get enough of what you *don't* really need.

You'll probably feel mightily inclined to skip this section of the book. Most people resist the personal requirements exercises with every fiber of their being. That's why I've made it as straightforward as possible for you to identify your top four personal requirements with the following quiz. Skip this section at your own risk: your needs only get worse when you deny or ignore them. Fulfill them and they handily disappear.

The easiest way to find out what your personal and emotional needs are is to take the Personal Requirements Quiz at Lifecoach .com, and it will tell you what your top four needs are. Write down your results, as the site won't remember what your answers are or who you are. If you don't have convenient access to a computer, then you can take the quiz with the paper-and-pencil version here. You'll have to devote a few extra minutes to tot up your score.

Personal Requirements Quiz

Instructions: For each of the scenarios that follow, if the situation rings true for you, check the corresponding need that most resonates with you. You are looking for the underlying need that drives the behavior. If the scenario isn't true for you or wouldn't apply to you, just skip it and move on to the next one. Similarly, if the scenario is true for you, but none of the needs listed sounds right, then skip it. You will probably skip quite a few that don't apply. On the other hand, don't worry if you have checked quite a few; that is perfectly normal, as we all have needs—some more than others. If you aren't sure about a question, ask a friend or family member who knows you well for an expert opinion.

1. You need a balance of work and play in your life in order to feel your best. If you work too much, you lose your sense of humor. If you play too much, you tend to get lazy or apathetic.

 Need for balance.

2. You are at a meeting in which two people start to argue. You feel uncomfortable and either try to smooth things over or shy away from the conflict.

☐ Need to be accepted/liked.

☐ Need for peace/harmony.

3. You are always doing favors for other people, even at your own expense.

 Need to be accepted/liked.

☐ Need to be appreciated.

☐ Need to be useful/needed.

4. You keep others at arm's length, because you don't want to get hurt.

 Need to be accepted.

☐ Need for safety/security.

5. You are the kind of person who goes out of your way to help others, even though you don't really have the time.

☐ Need for peace/harmony.

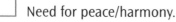 Need to be useful/needed.

☐ Need to be responsible/do the right thing.

6. You are constantly sending thoughtful notes, e-mails, or gifts to your colleagues.

 Need to be appreciated.

☐ Need to be accepted/liked/included.

☐ Need to be loved/cherished.

7. You hate being interrupted.

☐ Need to be heard/be listened to/communicate.

☐ Need for control/power.

8. People don't take what you say seriously.

☐ Need to be heard/listened to/understood.

9. You feel as if you are drowning—there are so many things vying for your attention that you have no time to pursue your true calling.

☐ Need for order.

☐ Need for balance/peace.

☐ Need for clarity.

10. You get irritable and cranky if your space is messy.

☐ Need for order/tidiness.

☐ Need for clarity.

11. You can't think clearly until your desk is cleaned off.

☐ Need for order/tidiness.

☐ Need for clarity.

12. You find yourself volunteering in the community homeless shelter, the church, or some other charitable organization, but your family doesn't appreciate all you do for them and the work you do in the community.

☐ Need to be needed/useful.

☐ Need to be appreciated/liked/approved of.

☐ Need to be responsible/have a cause or mission.

13. When your boss micromanages you, you feel suffocated. You think, "Why can't he/she trust me to do the job right?"

☐ Need to be independent/free.

☐ Need to be accepted/respected.

☐ Need for power/control/authority.

☐ Need to be right/deferred to.

14. It annoys you that your spouse or partner doesn't do things for you around the house, such as loading the dishwasher, unless you ask.

☐ Need to be cared for/supported/taken care of.

☐ Need to be loved/cherished.

15. You feel [fill in the blank] when your spouse or partner does small things around the house without your asking.

☐ Cherished/loved.

☐ Supported/taken care of.

16. You get anxious or restless when you don't have a project to work on. You enjoy pushing the limits to see what can be done.

☐ Need to accomplish/achieve.

☐ Need to be busy/work.

☐ Need to have a cause or mission/be responsible.

17. You get frustrated with bureaucracy that slows you down from getting results.

☐ Need to be free/independent.

☐ Need to accomplish/achieve.

☐ Need for power/control/authority.

18. You find yourself eating out of the fridge or in front of the TV even though you are not really hungry.

☐ Need to be cherished/loved.

☐ Need to be nurtured/supported/taken care of.

Need for security/safety.

 Need to be busy/work.

19. Your colleagues don't appreciate your point of view. You make a statement and nobody seems to hear you or understand you.

 Need to be heard/listened to/understood.

 Need to be recognized/get attention.

 Need to be appreciated/valued.

20. You always have to have the remote control.

 Need to be in control/power.

21. You can't stand it when your boss or colleague takes credit for what you've done.

 Need to be recognized/get credit/be noticed.

 Need to be appreciated/acknowledged.

22. You get very frustrated and/or upset if you don't get the recognition you deserve at work.

 Need to be recognized/noticed.

 Need to be appreciated/acknowledged/valued.

23. You feel lonely and removed from people and lose the desire for sex when you are not in a relationship.

 Need to be touched/held.

 Need to be loved/cherished.

24. You get furious, hurt, angry, or disappointed if you find out your coworkers make plans without inviting you, even if you know you can't attend. You still want to be invited regardless.

 Need to be included/liked.

25. You get really upset or annoyed if people do things or make plans without your knowledge.

 Need for power/control.

 Need to know/have clarity/be informed.

26. You have plenty of money in the bank, but you still don't feel secure. It is never enough somehow.

 Need for security/safety.

 Need for luxury/comfort.

27. Nobody loves losing, but you just can't stand it. You always have to win.

 Need to win/be the best.

28. People say that you are too opinionated or bullheaded, because you have to get your point across.

 Need to be heard/communicate.

 Need to be right/understood.

 Need to be responsible/do the right thing/do your duty.

 Need to win.

29. You have been known to tell your spouse or partner which way to turn out of the driveway.

 Need to control.

30. You like it when your boss, family, and friends approve of what you do and find it disturbing if they don't.

 Need to be accepted/approved of.

 Need to be appreciated/valued.

31. At parties and social gatherings, you need to be the center of attention and will tell jokes, sing songs, do silly stuff, or wear clothes that are guaranteed to attract attention.

Need to be recognized/get attention/be seen/be noticed.

32. You find it hard to do nothing and prefer, even when on vacation, to work on some project or another.

 Need to be useful/needed.

 Need to accomplish/achieve.

 Need to be busy/work.

33. If you don't have at least ten minutes of quiet time a day to yourself, the rest of the day is off kilter.

 Need for peace/balance/time alone.

34. It is vital for you to be in a position of power or authority. You need to be the one in charge whether at work or at home.

 Need for control/power/authority.

35. You can't be in a relationship unless your spouse or partner is faithful to you. An open marriage wouldn't work for you.

 Need to be in control/power.

 Need for responsibility/duty/loyalty.

 Need to be loved/cherished.

36. You are a perfectionist and can't abide it when things go afoul.

 Need for perfection/order.

37. You find yourself shopping several times a week. You get a high from shopping but then feel guilty afterward because you are buying on credit and know you can't pay off your credit card balance. Still you continue to shop, knowing you shouldn't.

 Need to be loved/cherished.

 Need for luxury/comfort/abundance.

38. You go into restaurants even when you are not planning to eat, just to see if anyone you know is dining there.

 Need to be seen/admired/recognized/known.

39. You can't sleep at night unless you've checked to make sure all the doors are locked.

 Need for safety/security.

40. You have a stockpile of canned goods and household supplies on hand.

 Need for luxury/comfort/abundance.

☐ Need for security/safety.

41. You feel compelled to always do the right thing, no matter what.

 Need for honesty/integrity.

☐ Need for duty/responsibility/justice.

42. Although you hate to admit it, you don't go on a second date with a person who didn't pick up the tab on the first date. You much prefer being treated and feel that people can't be all that interested in you if they didn't treat.

 Need to be supported/cared for.

 Need to be loved/cherished.

43. You love gossip. You can't resist passing on a juicy tidbit.

☐ Need to be recognized/get attention/be known.

☐ Need to be included/accepted/liked.

☐ Need to be heard/communicate/tell stories.

44. You naturally expect people to bring presents to your birthday party and feel miffed if someone doesn't bring one.

 Need to be cared for/supported.

45. You would never eat at a restaurant where the service is lousy, even though the food is superb.

 Need to be cared for/attended to/supported.

 Need for luxury/comfort.

46. You need to know that your lover, partner, or spouse desires you. It isn't enough that the person says so. You want demonstrable evidence before you are satisfied.

☐ Need to be supported/cared for.

☐ Need to be touched/caressed.

47. You tend to find yourself in messes or problem situations, but fortunately, someone usually comes along to rescue you or help you out.

☐ Need to be saved/supported.

48. You often ask leading questions in order to get a compliment, such as, "How do you like my dress/suit/hair?"

☐ Need to be loved/cherished/desired/adored.

☐ Need to be admired/recognized.

☐ Need to be complimented/appreciated.

☐ Need to be supported/encouraged.

49. You need a commitment before you can do your best work or be your best self—whether that is a job contract or a marriage contract.

☐ Need for security/safety.

☐ Need for clarity/certainty.

50. After a bad day, nothing makes you feel better than being held tenderly.

☐ Need to be touched/held.

☐ Need to be supported/cared for.

☐ Need to be loved/cherished/desired.

51. Life feels blah if you don't have a cause to rally behind.

☐ Need to be responsible/have a cause or mission.

Need to accomplish.

☐ Need to work/be busy.

52. You frequently write letters to the editor to correct injustices and wrongs.

☐ Need to have a cause or mission/duty/responsibility.

☐ Need to be right.

☐ Need for honesty/integrity.

53. You have to have the last word in an argument.

☐ Need to be right.

☐ Need to win.

☐ Need for power/control.

54. You can't stand being wrong.

 Need to be right.

☐ Need to win.

55. You go the extra mile when you have someone to encourage you.

☐ Need to be useful/needed.

☐ Need to be supported/encouraged.

56. Puns annoy you.

☐ Need for clarity/certainty.

57. You prefer to give rather than receive presents, because you don't want to feel obligated.

☐ Need to be free of obligation/independent.

58. You always have extra presents on hand to give for celebrations.

 Need to be free of obligation/independent.

59. You feel compelled to tell all and reveal everything even when it probably isn't in your best interest to do so at times.

☐ Need to share yourself/communicate/be heard.

☐ Need for honesty/integrity.

60. You refuse to take money from your friends or family, even though it would make your life easier.

☐ Need to be free of obligation/independent.

61. You can't stand taking orders from anyone.

☐ Need to be independent/free.

☐ Need for control/power.

62. If an error occurs, you quickly take responsibility, even if you were only partially at fault or not at fault.

☐ Need for duty/responsibility.

☐ Need for honesty/integrity.

63. You can't stand working on projects that you can't complete yourself.

☐ Need to accomplish.

☐ Need to control.

☐ Need for perfection/order.

64. You love lists and make them every day. You get joy from checking things off a list.

☐ Need for clarity.

☐ Need for order/checklists.

☐ Need to accomplish/achieve.

☐ Need to work/be busy.

65. If you don't meditate every day, you can't function at your peak.

☐ Need for peace/balance/time alone.

66. Your favorite days are jam-packed from start to finish. You relish the sense of accomplishment.

 Need to be busy/work.

 Need to accomplish/achieve.

 Need to be useful/needed.

67. You always go above and beyond the call of duty at both work and social occasions.

 Need to be useful/needed/indispensable.

Need to be valued/appreciated.

Need to be recognized.

Need to win/be the best.

68. You volunteer to cook dinners for the local church group or soup kitchen.

 Need to be needed/useful.

 Need to do the right thing/do your duty/be responsible.

Need to be valued/appreciated.

69. You donate a lot of your time and energy to charities or environmental organizations.

 Need to be needed/serve.

Need to be responsible/do your duty/do the right thing.

70. You need to have all the facts before you are comfortable making a decision.

Need to be informed/have clarity.

Need for security.

71. You tend to break the rules or make up your own rules.

 Need to be free/independent/unrestricted.

72. You are at a company banquet, and, rather than see all the leftovers go to waste, you ask the waitstaff to bring you a few containers so you can take the leftovers home.

☐ Need for security/safety.

☐ Need for comfort/abundance/luxury.

73. You will work extra hours if you know that your boss values your efforts.

☐ Need to be appreciated/valued.

☐ Need to win/be the best.

☐ Need to be approved of/liked.

☐ Need to be admired/recognized.

☐ Need to be supported/encouraged.

74. You would never ask for a doggie bag to take home the leftovers at a fancy restaurant. It just wouldn't look good or be cool.

☐ Need to be accepted/liked/respected.

☐ Need to be admired/recognized.

75. You prefer to eat food that comes in its own neat little package (yogurt, bananas, frozen dinners, instant oatmeal).

☐ Need for order/perfection.

76. You always balance your checkbook every month to the penny.

☐ Need for order/perfection.

☐ Need for clarity/certainty.

☐ Need for security/safety.

77. You tend not to speak up at a meeting if you know your views would cause an argument.

☐ Need for harmony/peace.

☐ Need to be approved of/liked.

78. You get really irritated when people don't confirm receipt of your e-mails or phone calls.

☐ Need for clarity.

☐ Need for acknowledgment.

☐ Need to be recognized.

☐ Need to achieve/accomplish.

79. You never leave the house without making sure your hair looks good, your grooming is complete, and you are well dressed.

☐ Need to be admired/recognized.

☐ Need for order/perfection.

☐ Need to be appreciated/complimented.

80. You proudly display all of your awards, plaques, certificates, and other forms of reward, recognition, or achievement in your home or office.

☐ Need to be important/recognized/admired.

☐ Need to be respected/accepted.

81. You feel treasured when your mate holds your hand, whispers sweet nothings in your ear, or makes other intimate gestures. If the person doesn't do these things, you feel that something is missing or that the person doesn't really like you.

☐ Need to be cherished/loved/treasured.

82. You love to get gifts. It doesn't have to be anything big; little presents and surprises are great! If you don't receive them from a loved one, you feel a bit neglected or unloved.

☐ Need to be cared for/supported.

☐ Need to be cherished/loved.

83. You enjoy parties and other social events on occasion but find you need some time alone to recharge. You may have to step outside for a breather at large social events.

☐ Need for peace/balance/time alone.

84. At holidays and other family gatherings, you get exhausted by the socializing and usually need to go out for a walk alone, or leave the room to read a book or watch TV.

☐ Need for peace/balance/time alone.

85. You don't like asking for directions and hate being told where to go by backseat drivers.

☐ Need to control.

☐ Need to be right.

86. You tend to get obsessed with whatever you are currently doing, but you find that you are actually happier and more productive if you balance work and play.

☐ Need for balance.

87. You don't like it when people touch you, even though you know they mean well or are just trying to comfort you.

☐ Need to control.

88. You love getting and giving hugs. You frequently reach out to touch someone's hand or arm, especially if the person is feeling sad or hurt.

☐ Need to be touched/held.

☐ Need to be loved/cherished.

☐ Need to be supported/taken care of.

89. When you throw a party or event, you always make sure to include everyone. You know how horrible it is to be left out.

☐ Need to be accepted/included.

☐ Need to be loved.

90. If you make a mistake, you take it very hard, even personally.

☐ Need to be right.

☐ Need for perfection/order.

☐ Need to be the best/win.

91. You need people to be perfectly clear and can't stand it when they mumble or ramble on.

☐ Need for clarity.

☐ Need for perfection/order.

92. You always say what is on your mind, even though it isn't always appropriate.

☐ Need for honesty/integrity.

☐ Need to be heard/communicate.

☐ Need to be right.

☐ Need to be responsible/do the right thing.

93. You get upset, concerned, or angry if someone doesn't fully communicate with you. You'd rather know the whole truth even if it is hard to hear.

☐ Need for honesty/integrity.

☐ Need for clarity.

94. When traveling, you take along all the comforts of home. In fact, you'd rather not travel if you can't be comfortable.

☐ Need for comfort/luxury.

95. You find you must keep the upper hand in most situations.

☐ Need to be in control/power.

☐ Need to be right.

☐ Need to win/be the best.

96. It's your way, or you'll find someone else who will do it your way.

☐ Need to be in control/power.

☐ Need to be right.

☐ Need to win.

97. You are known as the person who gets projects completed on time.

☐ Need to achieve/accomplish.

☐ Need to be recognized/known.

☐ Need to win/be the best.

☐ Need to work/be busy.

98. You don't respect people who are disorganized or messy.

☐ Need for order/perfection.

99. You must do your duty to your church, family, and country.

☐ Need for duty/responsibility.

☐ Need to be useful/needed/of service.

100. While some people seem to thrive on noise and chaos, you really can't think clearly or work effectively in a noisy environment.

☐ Need for peace/harmony/balance/time alone.

101. You always tell the truth, even though it may be easier or better not to.

☐ Need for honesty/integrity.

☐ Need to be responsible/do the right thing/seek justice.

102. You would never take even so much as a postage stamp from the workplace for personal use.

☐ Need for honesty/integrity.

☐ Need for duty/responsibility.

103. You make a concerted effort to fit in, regardless of the situation.

 Need to be accepted/liked/approved of/included.

104. A balanced life? That's for wimps!

 Need to be busy/work.

Need to accomplish/achieve.

Need to win/be the best.

105. You are overly generous and insist on treating friends and family, even though you really can't afford it.

 Need to be appreciated/liked/valued.

Need to be cherished/loved.

106. If you are out to dinner with a date, you insist on paying your way, even if your date wants to treat you.

 Need to be free of obligation/independent.

107. You have to be the boss, even if that means running your own business or company.

Need for power/authority/control.

 Need for freedom/independence.

108. You play full out to win. You don't let others beat you if you can help it.

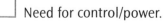 Need to win/be the best.

109. You aren't a very gracious loser. You really hate losing and have a hard time disguising the fact.

Need to win/be the best.

110. You prefer to facilitate a meeting, even if it isn't your meeting.

Need for control/power.

Need to be free/independent/unrestricted.

111. You don't feel loved if your partner doesn't cuddle up to you or caress you.

 Need to be touched/caressed.

112. When stressed, you usually pick up the phone and talk things over with a friend.

 Need to be heard/communicate.

113. Your friends say you have a fear of commitment, but you are really afraid of losing your independence or control.

 Need to be free/independent.

 Need for control/power.

114. You can't stand it if your partner reads the paper at mealtimes instead of talking or listening to you.

 Need to be heard/communicate.

115. You often reach out and touch people.

 Need to be touched.

116. People may say that it is the thought that counts, but you aren't impressed by small tokens or trinkets; you want your loved ones to give you high-quality jewelry or similarly expensive gifts.

 Need for luxury/abundance.

 Need to be cared for/supported.

117. You often walk up and give your partner a hug or shoulder massage while he or she is at the computer.

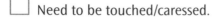 Need to be touched/caressed.

SCORING INSTRUCTIONS

Once you've finished, go back and add up how many times you've checked a particular need. For example, you've checked "approved of" five times, "cherished" twice, "control" three times, and so forth. The top four needs are the ones with the most checks. List your top four needs here:

MY TOP FOUR NEEDS

1. _____

2. _____

3. _____

4. _____

Congratulations! You have completed the first stage in getting your needs met: knowing what they are! Now let's get started working on them. At this point, you can refer to my website at Lifecoach.com or to my book *The Secret Laws of Attraction* for a more detailed treatment on the topic of personal requirements and needs. Once you fulfill your personal requirements, you'll find that they will "disappear" and you'll be immediately more attractive to current and potential employers. (There is nothing quite so repellent as an unmet need or personal requirement, after all!)

The Importance of Establishing Boundaries to Help You Achieve Your Personal Requirements

Now that you are fully aware of your top four personal requirements, your mission is to figure out how to satisfy them once and for all so that they effectively disappear. There are two aspects to this program, and while they are simple in principle, not everyone is prepared to execute them right off the bat. Trust me, though: you can do this.

First, you will expand your current boundaries, putting in place even bigger boundaries than you think you need. This will give you a greater sense of confidence and provide the added benefit of making you much more attractive to potential and current employers. We are naturally attracted to people with firm and clear boundaries, and we can't help but treat them with respect.

Second, you will learn how to ask directly for what you need. The best way to get your needs met is to be very specific and clear about what you want others to do and say to you and around you.

You will also create an automatic system to permanently and effortlessly satisfy your top four needs. Initially, there is work to do to put the system in place, but once it's established, you will reap the benefits for the rest of your life.

After completing the exercises in this section, you will be much more attractive to your current and potential employers (and your clients, if you own a business) and will have eliminated any neediness you might have had, whether you were consciously aware of it or not. The exercises are challenging, and you may resist doing them. I encourage you to do them regardless, especially if you don't feel like it—because that is precisely where you will gain the most benefit. If it were easy, you wouldn't have these needs in the first place, since you would have already fulfilled them. Put in the effort now and you will be rewarded with a profound sense of inner satisfaction and confidence that might have eluded you all your life.

Establish Bigger Boundaries than You Think You Need

The first action in getting your needs fulfilled is putting firm boundaries in place to make sure you are treated with respect. A lot of people find it hard to do this in the workplace, but without sufficient boundaries, you have no chance of fulfilling your needs permanently. To put it simply, a boundary is something that no one may do to you or around you. Most people already have boundaries in place, even if they aren't aware of them. For example, most of us have the boundary "People can't hit me." If someone hit us, we'd call the police and immediately end the relationship. This is a basic physical boundary. Some people, however, don't even have this boundary and stay in relationships in which they get hit or worse.

A bigger boundary than "No one may hit me" is "No one may yell at me." This is one step out from physical abuse to verbal abuse. One step further from "People can't yell at me" is "People can't make rude remarks or put-down comments about me." And then further still, "People can't give me unsolicited criticism." And even further, "People can't be angry or grumpy or argue with others around me."

You can set up any boundaries you wish. The bigger they are, the better. You need much bigger boundaries than you realize. In this exercise, you are going to specify ten boundaries you would like to have. Here are some common examples to get you started:

People can't violate my personal space.
People can't yell at me.
People can't give me unsolicited criticism.
People can't argue or fight in my presence.
People can't be crabby or grumpy around me.
People can't interrupt me.
People can't be late when meeting me.
People can't make rude or derogatory remarks or jokes about me or
    those around me.
People can't gossip around me.
People can't take advantage of me in any way.
People can't make racial jokes in my presence.
People can't waste my time
People can't use my things without my permission.
People can't lie to me.
People can't use foul language in my presence.
People can't be mean to me.
People can't ignore me.
People can't smoke in my home or around me.
People can't call me before nine A.M. or after nine P.M.
People can't interrupt my private or quiet time.
People can't give me work they should do themselves.
People can't belittle me or dismiss my remarks or opinions.

People can't snap at me.

People can't say things to me that make me feel stupid.

People can't take out on me feelings or issues that they have
concerning other people.

People cannot treat me inequitably.

You can choose any boundaries you like from the preceding list
and then add your own. Take a moment now to write down the
ten principal boundaries you want in your life:

MY TOP TEN BOUNDARIES

1. _____

2. _____

3. _____

4. _____

5. _____

6. _____

7. _____

8. _____

9. _____

10. _____

At this juncture, you are probably thinking, "Terrific! So, I've
got this new boundary: 'No one may raise his or her voice to me.'
Now what do I do about it?"

I have taught thousands of people an extremely effective four-
step communication model for establishing personal boundaries.
Before you begin, it helps if you understand that whenever someone crosses one of your boundaries, you've allowed the person
to do so. If you want the behavior to change, you need to let the

offender know about it graciously and firmly. Here is an example of how to stop the irritating or undesirable behavior in a graceful and effective manner. (Ladies, pay strict attention, since we tend to be particularly weak in this department!)

1. **The first step is to inform.** For example, "Do you realize that you are yelling?" Or, "Do you realize that your comment hurt me?" Or, "I didn't ask for your feedback." If the person continues with the unwanted behavior, take it to step two, but only after you've tried step one.
2. **Request.** Ask the person to stop. For example, "I ask that you stop yelling at me now." Or, "I ask that you give me only constructive feedback." If the person still doesn't get it and the behavior continues, try step three.
3. **Demand or insist.** "I insist that you stop yelling at me now." If the person still persists, take it to the next step.
4. **Leave (without any snappy comebacks or remarks).** "I can't continue this conversation while you are yelling at me. I am going to leave the room."

The secret to using this four-step model is to say everything in a neutral tone of voice. Do not raise your voice or let it fluctuate. You know when you've got a little fire or judgment in your tone. Remember, you are informing the other person, so keep it calm. Think of reciting each of the four steps in the same way you'd say, "The sky is blue." Keep in mind that successfully transitioning to a new career depends on creating an environment where you set these boundaries.

The Power of Establishing Boundaries at Work

How can you feel good about yourself if people are yelling at you all day? How can you feel appreciated if people criticize you? It is difficult to stay positive in these situations, especially if you are surrounded by criticism and negativity on a regular basis at home or at work. Even if it isn't personal, it just isn't acceptable for anyone to yell at you. Period.

When I worked at Chase Manhattan, I was taught that good customer service meant allowing irate customers to vent their frustration and anger and then offering them assistance. During my six years in retail banking, I listened to customers complain and yell every day. I was drained and exhausted at the end of each shift. A good day was one in which no one was upset—but people didn't often come into the bank if everything was OK. Were customers' reasons for being upset valid? Most often, yes, they were. Nevertheless, that didn't mean that as an employee, I had to be their sponge. This was a revelation to me, and to be honest, I was doubtful about whether boundaries could really work with the bank's customers. After all, the customer is always right.

To experiment, I put in place the basic boundary "People can't yell at me," and of course, I was tested that very day. From my office at the back, I could hear a man yelling at my customer service representative. I immediately thought, "Here goes." I walked out to the counter, where I saw that the source of the disturbance was a fortyish man reeking of alcohol. I approached him and in a neutral tone of voice said, "Do you realize you are yelling?" He was immediately flustered and, still yelling, said, "Of course. I'm not mad at you, though; I'm mad at the bank." "I understand," I said, "and you are still yelling. I ask that you stop yelling now so that we can help you." He mumbled something and walked to the teller window to conduct his business. When he had completed his transaction, he went back to the customer service desk and apologized for his behavior. Then he came to me and apologized as well. He left the bank a happy customer, and as far as I know, he never yelled in our branch again. It worked! And if it could work on an inebriated, belligerent stranger, then it could work on just about anybody.

I taught my entire staff the four-step model for installing boundaries and told them I would back them up as long as they kept their voices completely neutral and calm. I made it clear: if you raise your voice to the customer or get angry, you're on your own. The atmosphere of our branch transformed in one week. Customers started to treat staff with respect. The branch became a pleasant place to work and went from being a madhouse to being a quiet, tranquil setting. I knew we had succeeded when a gentleman came in to tell me he chose to bank at our branch because it had the best atmosphere in the entire neighborhood.

Are Boundaries Controlling?

Some people are concerned that having boundaries is about controlling others. This is a free country: aren't people entitled to do or say whatever they want as long as they're not breaking any laws? Yes, they are, and you are entitled to choose whether to stick around. Boundaries are not about controlling others. People will do what they want. Boundaries are about protecting yourself from others. When you inform people, you are simply teaching them how to treat you.

Everyone has different boundaries. It may not bother you if someone is late to meet you for an appointment, while that behavior may infuriate another person. Since people have different boundaries, it helps if you inform others of yours by gently telling them at the first infraction. Do not wait. It is much easier to stay calm and neutral if you address things immediately. Here is a sample dialogue:

"Do you realize you are ten minutes late?"

"So sorry; I was stuck in traffic."

"Of course, I know you respect my time."

Let the other party make a graceful retreat, and reinforce the behavior you want—respect. Do not gloss over this! Most people think, "Oh, this is the first time it's happened," or, "It is just a small thing, so I won't make a fuss." This is precisely the time to inform. You might say, "This is our first appointment, so you had no way of knowing how important timeliness is to me." Or more simply, "Do you realize you are fifteen minutes late?" Or, "I'd appreciate it if you'd show up on time." Think of it as holding up a mirror and reflecting back to people what they are doing.

Ninety-five percent of the population will get the message and show up on time for your next appointment. And for those who don't, take it to level two—request: "I request that you show up on time."

Most people make the mistake—especially women, since we have been raised to think we are being nice by not addressing something on the spot—of letting an infraction pass the first time. If you make it a point to address the behavior immediately, it is easier to do it in a neutral tone of voice without anger, resentment, or judgment. It is when we wait that all the anger builds and gets in the way of our ability to enjoy the relationship. People treat you the way they do because you have allowed them to do so, and you must take responsibility for how you have trained and educated people. Make it easy on yourself and give others, especially the ones you love, a chance to change their behavior. Inform and request a couple of times with friends and family before you move to demand and insist.

Do Boundaries Keep People at a Distance and Shut People Out?

While boundaries are permeable and allow us to let the "good guys" over the moat and into the castle, walls keep everyone out. If you don't have sufficient boundaries, you will get burned and will eventually put up walls to protect yourself. It is boundaries that enable us to really open up and be intimate, because we feel safe. The bigger your boundaries, the safer and more relaxed you'll feel, and the easier it will be to deeply connect with other people. And, I'd be surprised if you didn't already know that close and powerful relationships are the key to being successful in any line of work.

What if the four steps aren't working? Well, that means that you need to take the fourth step to the next level—leave the relationship. Ultimately, you can choose whether to continue that relationship. The good news is that I've never seen a case in which honoring one's boundaries was not rewarded. Sometimes friendships, relationships, or jobs will end, which creates the space for new and better people and opportunities to come into your life. I've had clients who decided to quit their jobs when all else failed. For example, one woman's boss just didn't get it and persisted in making sexist and derogatory remarks about her. She quit and found a new position in which people treated her with respect and she made more money to boot!

Boundaries are not about controlling people. We can't control others, and we can't force people to treat us in a certain way, but we can protect ourselves and choose what environments we stay in.

Will I Seem Too Demanding?

Don't be afraid of coming across too strong in using this model. Remember, to demand is the third step. First, inform and request before you demand. And if you do so in a neutral tone of voice (not a demanding or righteous tone), then you'll engender respect. Even if people choose not to honor your boundaries, they will probably respect you more for having them. Start with the boundaries that are most important to you, and work your way down.

Also, this isn't a one-way street. The flip side of boundaries is standards, the level of conduct to which we hold ourselves. It isn't appropriate to have the boundary "You can't yell at me" if you are yelling at others. Expanding your boundaries may have the benefit that you will also need to raise your personal standards of conduct.

One client was very demanding and had a hot temper. She used to yell at her colleagues and employees and expected them to put up with her bad behavior. Finally, one employee had strong enough boundaries and told her it wasn't OK for her to yell at him for any reason. He wouldn't stay in a job in which he was treated so badly. Whenever she raised her voice, he immediately informed her in a gentle but firm tone. She got the message, respected him for it, and learned how to control her temper. His boundary required her to raise her own standards of conduct.

Benefits of Having Strong Boundaries

Most people don't realize that they can greatly expand their boundaries, which will not only eliminate most of their professional problems, but it will also have the added benefit of improving their personal relationships as well. You will be much more attractive to powerful and influential people if you have strong boundaries.

1. **Setting bigger boundaries is well worth the effort because of the rich rewards: people will respect you.** We respect people who have big boundaries, and we do not respect those who don't (those are the "doormats" we walk over). We are often tempted to abuse those without boundaries. Perhaps this trait is part of the survival-of-the-fittest concept—animals casting out the weak and sick so the stronger members can thrive. As with other animals, we humans can sense boundaries immediately. This ability is beneficial. Often, after you install a new boundary, such as "People can't criticize me," either you'll be tested right away or no one will violate it. Most people instinctively sense your new boundaries and don't go there; in this example, it's likely no one will criticize you anymore thanks to the powerful new aura that you'll be projecting.

2. **Only those with strong boundaries get promoted.** We are naturally attracted to the people we like and respect—the people who have a sense of dignity and self-esteem. When you have strong boundaries, it is easier to attract the right opportunity and get promoted. Nobody respects or promotes a doormat. If you feel you are being taken advantage of at work or are not being treated properly, then you are missing some boundaries. Without them, it is impossible to break through to the upper levels of management. You don't see people criticizing or making derogatory remarks to the senior executives. It just isn't done thanks to the huge boundaries those executives have in place. The sooner you establish bigger boundaries, the more likely you are to get promoted.

3. **Your needs will diminish and your confidence will increase.**
   Now that you have written down your top ten boundaries and have
   started informing those around you, you will find that you won't
   need as much. It is often our inadequate boundaries that create
   need in the first place. For example, if you have the need to be
   respected, and your friends and colleagues constantly show up late
   when meeting you or interrupt you when you are speaking, you
   may feel that they disrespect you. Once you have the boundaries
   in place, people will naturally treat you better. The better we are
   treated by others, the better we feel about ourselves and the more
   self-assured and confident we become. This process is normal,
   natural, and completely effortless. All it takes is a concerted effort
   up front to retrain and educate those around you on how you
   wish to be treated from now on. Once you do this, you'll learn that
   it then is easier to ask people to do specific things to fulfill your
   personal requirements. For more information on exactly how to
   do this, read *The Secret Laws of Attraction*, where I have covered
   the topic extensively and outlined in detail what you can ask your
   friends and family to do to fulfill your personal needs.

Design Your Ideal Life

Do not take life too seriously. You will never get out of it alive.

—ELBERT HUBBARD

Good. Now that you have perfected your present job (even if it is the temp position you've taken to make ends meet while you look for the real career you want) and figured out your priorities and personal requirements, you are in a much better place to attract new and better professional opportunities. This brings up the question of what it is you really want to do. Maybe you already know the answer, or maybe you have no clue. In any case, whether you are starting your own business or looking for another career, the next step is to design your ideal life. Where do you want to live? What sort of people or community do you favor? How would you like to spend your time? Your first order here is to let go of media-inspired visions of success. You won't need the big house, fancy car, or expensive clothes if your ideal career is to teach English to children in Africa.

As a coach, I can cite several excellent examples of colleagues who modeled putting one's life ahead of a fancy lifestyle. They made sure that their careers supported their ideal lives brilliantly. Thomas Leonard, the founder of Coach U, bought a big RV and traveled all over the United States while coaching from phone and computer—truly the first portable coach! And Jeffery Raim, one of the first presidents of the International Coach Federation, used to coach on Mondays and take the rest of the week off to ski. Most people do it the other way around: they get a fancy lifestyle and then have to work at a job they don't particularly enjoy to support that lifestyle. You may need to ditch the lifestyle to get the life you *really* want.

While most of my clients are more prosperous after they orient their lives around their natural abilities, strengths, values, and passions, a few people choose careers that are personally rewarding but are not necessarily financially rewarding. I wouldn't say that it is always true that if you do what you love, the money will follow—van Gogh is a case in point. More often than not, though, my clients end up making more money than when they were slogging it out doing something they didn't really enjoy—sometimes lots more money! The following are some assignments and games to get you thinking outside of the box and designing the life you've secretly dreamed of. Have some fun with these exercises!

If Money Were No Object

Every once in a while, it is a good idea to break through our limited thinking about what is possible. Now that you want to change careers, it is the perfect time to think about what your ideal life and work would be. I usually do this exercise at family get-togethers with my mother and sisters after dinner. Here is how it goes: Ask your friends and family members the question, "If you had all the money you could ever want, what would you do?" Then go around the room and see what everyone says.

> *I only want enough to keep body and soul apart.*
>
> —DOROTHY PARKER

Alternatively, you can simply take out a pen and write down at least one hundred things you would do, be, or have if money were no object. You don't need to limit yourself in any way.

An interesting follow-up question you could add is, "If you had only six months to a year to live, what would you do?"

Or, to do this privately, try the "genie game" instead: Imagine you are walking on the beach and stumble on a bottle. You pick it up, and out pops a genie, who hands you a piece of paper and a pen and says, "You can have everything and anything you want to do, be, or have. Just write it down on this piece of paper in the next five minutes." Do this now! There are no limits. If you want to fly to the moon, no problem. If you want to become president, no problem. If you have fantasized about becoming a famous actor, write it down. If you have always wanted to own a yellow Mini Cooper, put it down. If you want a house in the mountains or on the beach, put it down. Also include things you want to experience: If you want to visit the Pyramids in Egypt, walk the Great Wall of China, see the Grand Canyon, or learn to dance the salsa, commit it to writing.

Nothing is impossible, too expensive, or too difficult. Write down every single thing that you can think of as quickly as you can, without judging or censoring yourself. Your choices may sound crazy or impossible, but this isn't about being logical, reasonable, or sensible. This is about throwing caution to the wind and writing down your wildest dreams. Try to come up with at least one hundred different things you would like to do, be, and have. Write down every single wish, desire, fantasy, dream, or hope that you can possibly think of. Most people start writing and soon get stuck and can't think of anything else. Keep writing past this point. Stretch yourself to come up with even more entries— stuff that you thought you could never have or become but that you secretly want. Don't worry: you don't have to actually do any of these things. The purpose of this exercise is to bust through your limited beliefs about what you think you can and should do in this lifetime. Most people play way too small!

Now that you have your list in hand, let's narrow it down to what you really want. Pick the top ten things you really want to be, do, or have in this lifetime. Imagine that you are on your deathbed looking back on your life: what would you regret *not* having done? Write this on your top ten list in the space provided in this section. Or, if long-range thinking leaves you blank, ask yourself, "What would I do if I had six months to a year to live?" Pick out the top ten things and record them here.

A little aside about regret: we usually regret not having done something we wanted to do or not having said something we should have said—forgiving someone, apologizing to someone, spending more time with loved ones, having a unique experience in life, or fulfilling a dream that we've secretly been nurturing. I've yet to hear of anyone on his or her deathbed regretting not having bought that diamond Rolex watch or fancy sports car.

IF MONEY WERE NO OBJECT, I WOULD

1. _____

2. _____

3. _____

4. _____

5. _____

6. _____

7. _____

8. _____

9. _____

10. _____

"If Money Were No Object" Exercise—Real-Life Stories

Thomas Leonard, the founder of CoachU.com, sold his house in Colorado, bought an RV, and traveled around the country while he coached and set up his phone-based coach-training program. He traveled and coached like this for more than a year, keeping his costs to a bare minimum so that he could invest his time, energy, and money in starting a coach-training company. It paid off when he later sold the company for $2 million.

Karen Kingston, the author of *Creating Sacred Space with Feng Shui*, spends half her time in England and half her time in Bali.

One client, Ali Brown, who was from New York, dreamed of living in California. She quit her ad-writing job in New York City and started her own business doing copy writing on a freelance basis. She decided to move to Los Angeles and set up her business where she wanted to be. She rented an apartment by the sea with a pool and worked on creating a perfect body, took acting classes, and even did some commercials. She then self-published a book online and is now a multimillionaire teaching other business owners how to be successful.

Timothy Ferriss, author of *The 4-Hour Workweek*, has set up his business so that he can work out for a few hours every day and is free to travel around the world learning new languages and taking tango lessons in Brazil. He didn't start out this way: at first, he worked every hour of the day managing and attending to all the minute details of his business. It was only when he learned to delegate and outsource that he started making serious money and started having time for his ideal life. His life is proof that working harder doesn't necessarily mean more money. In fact, the less he worked, the more money he made. Very inspiring! If you start by figuring out what your ideal life is, you'll save yourself all the grief that Ferriss went through when launching his business.

> *Never keep up with the Joneses. Drag them down to your level. It's cheaper.*
>
> —QUENTIN CRISP

Another client, a chiropractor, hired me because he didn't know whether he should expand his current practice. I asked him how he liked to spend his free time, and he replied that he enjoyed biking up the local mountain and reading books at the top, as well as hanging out with his ten-year-old son. Not very expensive activities. Given that context, he opted to downsize his business, simplifying his life so he'd have more time with his son and time on the mountain. Much to our amazement, he ended up clearing a larger profit with the smaller business and had more time than ever. Bigger business doesn't always lead to more profits—in his case it just led to more hassles!

Melissa Todd, whose "Success Story" is featured in the first chapter, was working as the HR manager in a law firm, and although her boss and colleagues valued her highly, her passion in life has always been dogs. She dreamed about setting up her own business around working with dogs. While still employed full-time, she started building her own business in the evenings. Her goal was to create the best doggie day-care service in Austin, Texas, called Hip Hounds. Because she was working full-time and couldn't be at the business during the day, she had to hire and train staff and managers right from the start.

Melissa used a business loan to fund the venture the first year, and after year two, she was making enough money to quit her day job at the law firm. Melissa was pretty busy during that period, but having a job helped get her through the toughest two years—the stage in which most businesses fail due to insufficient capital, because they just don't have enough income yet to get off the ground. Also, she had to delegate right away and set in place systems to manage her team virtually. Thanks to these accomplishments, she can run her doggie day care while sampling the wines of Napa Valley—another favorite pastime. Melissa's story is an outstanding example of what it looks like to orient your entire life around your top core values!

What Would Your Ideal Day Look Like?

If you are struggling to create the ideal life, then start with one ideal day. Write down what that day would look like from the moment you wake up in the morning to the moment you go to sleep at night. Be as detailed as possible. One of my clients did this exercise and realized that he could live his ideal day right then. When you're done, see if you can expand this description into a full week of ideal days. Next: start incorporating as many elements of your ideal day as you can into your life right now. If you want to wake up to a butler coming in with croissants and

> *There must be more to life than having everything.*
>
> —MAURICE SENDAK

coffee, don't let it bother you if you don't have the butler yet—start with the croissants and coffee.

MY IDEAL DAY

_____

_____

_____

_____

_____

One of my clients who performed this exercise realized that the perfect way to start the day was to go outside on her deck overlooking beautiful woods with a hot cup of tea and a fresh-baked blueberry muffin and write in her journal. She baked a batch of muffins and put them in the freezer, bought a journal, and got started! This fabulous beginning to her day led to a wonderful new career opportunity. She discovered a passion for writing, started writing articles for publication in magazines, and is now working on a book. Even if you can't put all the elements in place right now, start with the ones you can and you'll soon be adding in the missing bits.

We often get so wrapped up in our careers that they consume our entire lives. This may be just fine if you love what you do, but it certainly isn't fine if you don't. Start with your ideal life, and then look for the career that supports that life. This approach will save you a lot of hassle down the line. If pursuing this course means you need to downsize dramatically, then start downsizing. Your life is more important than any lifestyle, and although there may be some initial flack from your family, after a period of adjustment, your whole family will be happier when you are happy.

Another client was a high-powered, six-figure earning executive who used to travel all the time for his work and rarely had time for his family. He packed it all in for a job as a policeman, which was something he'd always wanted to do, but felt he would disappoint his family if he took a much lower-paying job. It meant selling the big house, getting rid of the third car, and moving into a more modest house. His wife supported him in doing this, and they are all happier now that he isn't so stressed and has time to spend with his kids. The kids didn't care about the big house, they just wanted to play with their father. The things that often matter most to people are usually free.

Make a Collage

Still struggling? Take a tip from interior designers. Flip through an assortment of magazines and cut out anything that jumps out at you as something that would be part of your ideal life. You can paste these images up on a poster board or whiteboard with some glue or rubber cement. Make a collage, and hang it up so you see it every day as a visual reminder of what you are working to create. Visual reminders are powerful tools!

Write the Ideal Job Description

Now that you've come up with your ideal life, let's start getting clearer on your actual job description. It is important that you write down your ideal job, career, or work in as much detail as you possibly can. Imagine that you are composing the ultimate classified ad, one that would leap off the paper and grab you—the very description should set your heart racing as you read it. You may be thinking, "This job doesn't even exist!" Don't fret: that may well be the case, and you may just be the person to invent it.

My profession, life coaching, has been around for just a little more than a decade, although sport coaching has been around much longer. When I started coaching and told people I was a coach, they always asked what sport. Now people say, "Oh, yeah, I know a life coach. Her name is . . . " —almost everyone these days has heard of or even knows a life coach. It didn't take long for this still relatively new profession to grow in leaps and bounds. As the world and technology are changing, new needs are developing, and whole new professions that never existed before are emerging. Not long ago, I was listening to a radio program on which a young woman was bemoaning the loss of her job and how was she ever going to find another job in her field . . . blah, blah. When I heard her say that her job was a Web designer, I had to laugh out loud. It wasn't as if she'd descended from a long line of Web designers, and this was all there was for her to do in the world. Let's face it: the Web itself is relatively new in the grand scheme of things, let alone the Web design profession. So, don't be concerned as you write your ideal job description for a job that doesn't exist. It soon will!

The one thing that remains certain is change, and rapid change at that. We are out of the industrial age (the last of the U.S. car manufacturers is closing down as I write) and into the information age. If your ideal career doesn't exist right now, create it. That advice isn't as crazy as it sounds. Many things that I formerly never thought would be possible are now ancient history. I never imagined, for instance, that the cold war would end and that the Berlin Wall would come down in my lifetime. The computers that once took up entire buildings are now so small that you can carry them in a pocket. You can communicate instantly and for free through the Internet to people all around the world—and do that by video now too with YouTube! At the same time, there are simplistic concepts we have been unbelievably slow to connect: for example, computers existed before someone had the brilliant—and incredibly obvious—idea of putting wheels on suitcases. The gods must be laughing their heads off at that one! In sum, there has been no better time to invent a career or a business completely tailored to your unique talents and abilities.

Again, be as precise as possible. What sort of working environment would you prefer? Do you like to work in an office setting with other people? If so, describe the scene in vivid detail: what would your office look like? Maybe, instead, your ideal is to work out of doors all day or to travel for your work? Be specific so that you don't miss the mark. One friend said that he wanted his work to take him all over the world; he is now an investment banker, and he travels all the time but rarely gets out of the airport or hotel conference room to see the city he is in. Not my idea of enjoyable travel! What income would you like? Who would you like to work with, and who would you like to be your customer base? Young kids, babies, adults, elderly populations, professionals, academicians? Do you want to work with your hands, or do you prefer to work with abstractions? List everything you can possibly think of. The more specific, the better. This assignment can take the form of bullet points, a real classified ad, or just a long descriptive account. Don't worry if it doesn't sound practical, possible, or sensible. Don't worry if you need retraining or more education to do it. We'll get to that later. For now, just jot down a quick draft of what you think would be ideal. You'll fine tune this later in Step 6. The point of this exercise is to start writing down what you already know you'd like to do, and then we'll expand and refine it.

MY IDEAL JOB DESCRIPTION

_____

_____

_____

_____

_____

_____

Great! Now that you've outlined your ideal job description, you'll find it is much easier to articulate what you really want to potential employers. Being armed with this knowledge also makes it much easier for you to find or create the career you really want, as opposed to settling for what is available. Some clients are delighted to discover that the ideal life is within reach with just a few small changes. Others need to do a major overhaul and change directions completely. One client, Nadine, realized that she didn't like her job, her relationship, or the city in which she was living. In one fell swoop, she quit her job, broke up with her boyfriend, packed her bags, and moved to Chicago for a totally fresh start.

Most people don't need to make such dramatic life changes, but if you do, why waste another minute in the wrong life?

While you are changing careers, you might as well take the time to consider all aspects of your ideal life. After all, if you've always dreamed of living in New York, it won't do you any good to be taking a job in Kansas City. Your job is just one aspect of living an ideal life. If you are miserable in cold climates, you won't want that job in Alaska, no matter how rewarding it may sound!

SUCCESS STORY

The Assistant Ad Writer Who Quit and Became a Multimillionaire

Ali Brown is currently the founder and CEO of Ali International at alibrown.com, but she started out as an assistant ad writer. She quit her job, started working as a freelancer, and is now, ten years later, a multimillionaire who has just launched her own magazine. Her magazine is *Ali*, geared to female business owners and entrepreneurs. She also has more than forty thousand members in her online programs.

I worked with Ali when she first started a decade ago. When I met her in a networking group in New York City, she hated her job working in a small advertising company. She had been a job-hopper, jumping every two years to a new position. She was restless. She was always wanting and trying to make changes to help the company become more successful but was constantly told just to focus on her current tasks. She began to think she was unemployable and kept looking for a situation that would be the right fit. Her last staff job was with that ad agency—although she was unhappy there, she was allowed to work with clients and got the feel of running a business.

Her salary had been meager for New York City at $35,000 a year. She said that she used to envy a freelancer for the company who could come and go as he pleased. One day, inadvertently, his invoice for services ended up on her desk, and she was shocked to see that his bill for one project was more than her total annual salary! That, Ali said, was a real eye-opener: "I didn't realize that you could make that much money as a freelancer." The prospect of having freedom and money appealed to her.

Plus, she said, her bosses didn't seem especially brilliant, so she figured, "OK, if these knuckleheads can do this and turn over a million dollars a year, then maybe I can do this on my own and at least make enough just to live on by myself."

She quit her job when an opportunity to work part-time as a freelancer for another firm appeared. This new flexible position was her safety cushion—it covered the rent while she started her own business.

Talane interviews her client, Ali:

How did you start your career reinvention?

I had no clients, but I just couldn't work for anyone else anymore. I was terrified, but the excitement was greater. There was no reason not to be scared, as I had no savings, but I thought about the worst thing that could happen, and that would be to move back home and live with my parents. I remember meeting a college friend for drinks the day I quit my job. When I announced I had just quit that day, her face blanched, and she asked, horrified, "But what will you do?" I told her I was starting my own business. "But how can you do that?" I had no idea really, but I didn't let that stop me. I started my business on two credit cards and had to pay for your coaching on credit.

Why did you hire a coach?

I had no one to talk to about what I was doing who would believe in me, except for you. You were the catalyst that gave me the confidence that I could do it. I had no voice in my life of someone who could say, "You can do this." I remember once I couldn't withdraw $20 from the ATM because my balance was $18.56. That was a real low point. And there was one week that I was trying to learn QuickBooks and had no money, and I had the thought, "I'm not smart enough to do this: I must not be smart enough to have my own business. Maybe I should go find a job." But you pointed out that I didn't need to do the bookkeeping and persuaded me to hire a virtual assistant before

I thought I could afford one. She has since bought into the business and is now my partner!

What is the biggest transition you've made?

When we are in traditional jobs and in school, we are taught to work our way up one step at a time. When you work for yourself, there are no rules and no limits. There is no reason why I should do a magazine: I have no magazine experience; it is an outrageous move to start a new magazine in the middle of a deep recession when other magazines are going out of business. To me it is play. When I was eleven years old once, playing in my room, I created a magazine called Cool Girl by cutting out pictures from other magazines and pasting them into my own.

And yes, I'm scared. But when I really set my mind to doing something, the universe supports me. Miraculous stuff happens. You are the one who taught me about the laws of attraction long before anyone had ever heard of The Secret. I have no consideration that I could fail. That just isn't an option. I went from producing a 4-page printed newsletter to a 124-page glossy magazine. I also made the leap from charging $19,000 a year for mentoring business owners to charging $100,000 a year. And I did it. I have ten clients at that rate now. You don't have to move up incrementally when you own your own business.

Now is a great time for women to be going into business on their own, because they can create the business around who they are and their values. This is a great time for women because they are great at communication, relationships, working with purpose, and honoring their values. Many women take their hobbies and make them into viable businesses.

If you could do anything differently now, what would you do?

I would have hired a life coach sooner, while still working in that job I hated, and created a more moderate transition plan. It would have helped to have had some savings, for starters. Also, I had no idea how to get clients; I would have done a bit of research on how to do that first instead of just jumping in. Ironically, that is what I started teaching others—how to get clients by using the Internet. It is what I needed to learn to be successful myself.

What advice do you have for those who are stuck in jobs they hate and are afraid to make that leap?

When you are stuck in a job, you can't necessarily see the next step to take; you just have to take it first. You don't see all the steps lined out in front of you, but as you make the first step, the second step reveals itself. I never know exactly how I'm going to do it. Listen, do your homework. You have to make decisions not from where you are, but from where you want to be. I would ask myself, "What would Ali, the six-figure business owner, do?" She would raise her rates and probably wear a nicer pair of pants! I remember when I was looking for a new apartment after my divorce and the real estate agent was showing me the one-bedroom apartments, but I thought that it would be really great to have a second bedroom for my office so that I wasn't squashed into a corner of the living room. It was $400 more for the two-bedroom apartment with water views, which was a lot of money for me then. I made the leap and took the two-bedroom even though it scared me and then attracted the clients and the extra revenue needed to pay for it.

What is the best outcome of all this?

Peace of mind. I can take care of myself. I can take care of my mom. The influence I have on the world to impact people, who in turn impact others: it is the ripple effect.

See alibrown.com for a look at Ali's website.

Identify Your Natural Talents and Abilities

Capacities clamor to be used and cease their clamor only when they are well used.

—ABRAHAM MASLOW

The more people I coach, the more firmly I believe that we are all born with certain innate abilities and talents. We are not lumps of clay at birth waiting to be molded into shape by our parents and environment. We arrive on this planet preformed to a fairly large extent. For example, from the age of six, we can be tested for the three abilities that make for musical talent (rhythm memory, pitch discrimination, and tonal memory). And, by the age of fifteen, your brain is pretty much set into the patterns that will stick for the rest of your life. After this age you can take a computerized assessment that reveals whether you have the ability to see things in three dimensions (helpful if you want to be an architect). Tests can indicate whether you are a visionary and able to imagine the future or whether you are a tactician and adept at getting the immediate task at hand completed.

> *Most people think they know what they are good at. They are usually wrong.*
>
> —PETER DRUCKER

Do you have the capacity to do higher mathematics, medicine, architecture, writing, performance? Some people are born with a set of abilities that match up nicely to certain professions. If you can't imagine things in three dimensions, you may find that fields such as engineering or architecture just aren't for you. Some people need to work with their hands to feel satisfaction in their endeavors; they need a tangible end result, or else they may feel that they work all day and produce nothing, even if they actually are getting abstract tasks done. Others have such strong musical abilities that they need to include music in their lives or learn to play an instrument before they will be happy. Do you know if you are a specialist by nature and like to go into depth on one topic or field or are a generalist and know a little bit about a lot of different subjects? It isn't always obvious. I used to think I was a generalist and was good at a lot of different things, but after taking a computerized assessment, I was surprised to discover that I'm really a specialist. I know a lot about coaching and things pertaining to human growth and development, but I don't know much at all about history, for example.

> *The most important thing is to be whatever you are without shame.*
>
> —ROD STEIGER

You may be one of the lucky ones who stumbled on your natural talent early in life and have focused on that. Still, even the most exciting jobs can become tiresome in time. One of my English clients was a real rock star, and after being a professional musician and playing in a band traveling and performing around the world for years, at forty-something he was ready to try something new. His girlfriend had a career in the United States, and he wanted to do something that he could do in the States as well that would enable him to follow her there. Yes, he had toured America with his band, but he now wanted to do something completely different. It was a case of been there, done that. He was ready for a change. He took The Highlands Program, and we weren't surprised to see that he had all three of the abilities that make for musical talent. We already knew that would happen, but what was interesting was that he had the right makeup to become a registered nurse. He loves to take care of people, and he favors hands-on work. Nursing would be ideal, as there is a demand for nurses in the United States, which would make it easier for him to get into the country. He was pleased to discover this, as nursing had been one of the careers he was considering.

So, even if you already know what *some* of your talents are, you may not have a handle on *all* of your inherent talents and hardwired abilities. Some people never even have a chance to discover what their true talent is because they become skilled at something that is reasonably enjoyable and for which they get paid well—too well to justify a switch to something that may be more personally fulfilling.

Some people don't start doing what they really want to do until they have retired. You don't have to wait. Start now. The sooner you start, the better your chances are of being successful at it, because you'll have more time to develop your natural talents and reach mastery. Or, you may be like me: I didn't know that I was a natural coach until I was twenty-nine. Also, although I had vague notions of writing westerns after I retired, I had no idea that the ability to write was hardwired in. It is easier for me to coach, speak, and write than it is for others, simply because my brain is designed for those tasks. Oddly enough, even though I was a successful manager at the bank and got good evaluations, management turns out to be one of my weakest areas. I was astounded to discover that something I thought was a strength, something at which I had proved successful, was something I shouldn't be doing. No wonder I felt I hadn't tapped into my full potential—I hadn't!

If you feel that something is missing or that you haven't tapped into your full potential, you are right. I'm aghast at how many people prefer to take antidepressants or numb themselves with alcohol or other substances to stay in a job they don't like because it pays well. What chance for happiness do you have if you are stuck doing something you detest for eight or more hours a day? If you aren't happy in your current job, don't try to ignore your unhappiness or dull it with drugs. Your displeasure is your body and mind's way of saying, "Get me out of here!" If you invest a bit of time and money into discovering your hidden talents and your passions, you'll soon be a much happier camper, because you'll be getting a natural high from doing work you love to do. You won't have to hit the snooze alarm fifteen times either, because when your job is exciting and interesting, you'll want to get out of bed and get to it.

Our inherent abilities and natural talents are so much a part of our makeup that they can be like breathing; we may take them completely for granted and not even recognize them as special talents or abilities. I, for one, had no idea I could coach people. Even when my own life coach told me I'd be a good coach, I was skeptical. I went into the field reluctantly and cautiously. Fair enough, given that at the time, life coaching was a completely new field; I was sensible enough not to throw out a good job at the bank, even though I wasn't happy there, for what I thought might end up being some fly-by-night profession. Thankfully, I learned that coaching, speaking, and writing are all among my top talents. It is immensely helpful to know how your brain is hardwired. I learned all sorts of interesting nuggets in addition to the fact that management isn't a natural talent. I even now understand such former mysteries as why I can't do a line dance but like to partner dance. I can't even clap in time—no rhythm memory. This is also why I've always been an enthusiastic but uncoordinated athlete.

We can't be good at all things, and if we could, that would become a problem too, because most jobs require only one or two distinct abilities. If you are multitalented, then it is difficult to feel completely satisfied in one job. Many people who have numerous talents find they hop from job to job looking for that elusive satisfaction, when in fact they simply need to add a variety of tasks to the current job.

I have a sister who has never been particularly happy in any of the jobs she has had, and that is primarily due to the fact that she has so many natural talents and abilities that no ordinary job can possibly fulfill them all. If you have a strong ability, it will demand to be expressed. If you don't express it, you'll feel frustrated and unsatisfied with your work. The solution is to identify all your driving abilities and then find ways to fulfill them outside of work if they can't be expressed in your career. Or design a career that uses them all—which is what I have done. I do a bit of writing, a bit of coaching, and a bit of speaking all under the umbrella of life coaching.

How Do You Discover Your Natural Talents?

There are a number of ways to identify your unique talents and natural abilities. You might find that after doing one of the following exercises it will become crystal clear to you what you are meant to do. On the other hand, you might find it helps to do all of the exercises that follow to get an overall picture and see where that leads. If, after completing this chapter, you still don't feel entirely clear, then I'd recommend taking one of the excellent computerized assessments online, as that typically does the trick.

> *I always wanted to be somebody, but I should have been more specific.*
>
> —LILY TOMLIN

Interview Your Friends, Family, and Coworkers

Usually it is much easier for someone else to identify your natural abilities. When I work with clients on computerized assessments, people are more accurate about identifying what they are not good at than what they are good at. You may be well aware, for instance, that you hate doing the taxes or accounting and have no head for numbers, but you may not be aware that you are an excellent facilitator. We are often the last ones to realize what our talents are, precisely because they are so natural to us. A fish doesn't realize it is a brilliant swimmer, since it is always in water and is just doing its thing.

Sometimes we make the erroneous assumption that because we can do something easily and well or because something sounds like great fun, it can't be real work or become a profitable business. If we are having fun or doing a task with ease, it doesn't feel like "hard work." This response may have to do with the Puritan work ethic: if it is fun, you shouldn't be doing it for work. This is a common subconscious belief. I know numerous coaches who have difficulty charging for their coaching because they love doing it so much and get so much fun out of it. If you have the belief that work must be difficult and challenging before you can be paid for it, then the place to start is getting rid of that negative, limiting belief!

> *The best mirror is an old friend.*
>
> —GEORGE HERBERT

My company just lost a prospective client because he was so convinced work had to be hard and a struggle that instead of building a business around his dreams, he decided to hire a coach who would strictly hold him accountable to his weekly goals and actions in commercial real estate, which he hated. In my company, we work with dreams. If you hate doing something, you'll never ever be the best at it. There will always be someone who loves doing the same thing and will soon beat you to that client or prospect. Now is the perfect time to figure out what you'd really love to do!

Ask as many friends, family members, teachers, coaches, and colleagues as you can get your hands on the six questions listed in this section. Take notes on what they say, or provide them a photocopy or e-mail of the questions to answer in writing. Do not make any comments or judgments about their responses. Your task is to simply gather as much information from as many people as you can and graciously thank them for their time and input. If you interview them in person or by phone, imagine you are an independent journalist gathering important information for a story about a very interesting person (you!). You can say things such as, "Hmmm . . . that is interesting. Tell me why you think that." Then jot down the answers. Do *not* get into an argument or a debate. You will tabulate all the data afterward and then see what common themes, if any, appear. Ask people you've known for ages and also people you've recently met, as the two groups may have different perspectives.

If you e-mail this list and do not receive a response, be sure to follow up with a phone call or gentle e-mail reminder and include a deadline. For example, "It would be great if you could get this to me in the next two weeks." People will want to give these questions some serious thought and may need some time to work on them. If you still don't get a reply from someone, call the person and ask if you can do the interview by phone, or just ask someone else. Strive for five to ten or more replies. Then take a few minutes to interview yourself as well.

SIX INTERVIEW QUESTIONS FOR YOUR FAMILY, FRIENDS, AND COWORKERS

1. What do you think is my greatest strength?
2. What is my biggest weakness? (Ask this because typically, the flip side of our greatest strength is one of our primary weaknesses. For instance, the person who has a talent for seeing the big picture is usually not good at details; if you can readily imagine five to ten years into the future, you may not be so proficient at dealing with the task at hand today and find that you procrastinate.)
3. What do you see as my special talent, ability, or gift?
4. What do I do naturally and effortlessly that is special?
5. If I were on the cover of a magazine, what magazine would it be, and what would the article be about? (This is a really fun one!)
6. When am I most fully expressing this talent, gift, or ability?

INTERVIEW QUESTIONS FOR YOURSELF

1. What things do I frequently get complimented on or praised for?
2. What do people ask me to help them with or do for them?
3. What is it that I do so well that people say I should get paid for it?
4. What am I good at? (List everything—and it should be a long list—that you are good at doing, from typing to fixing things to listening; write down every single skill that you have.)
5. What did I do for fun as a child? (This is an excellent question to ask your parents when you are interviewing them about your strengths and abilities.)

Draw Inspiration from Your Childhood

For inspiration, think back to what you used to do for fun as a child. You were pure and innocent then, and you naturally played games and did things that you enjoyed. What were those various pastimes? In the space provided in this section, write down everything you did for pure fun as a child. If you can't remember, ask your parents, review old home movies, dig out the early photo albums, or retrieve that old box of toys from the attic and see if these items remind you of what you used to love.

Revisiting your childhood this way is more revealing than you may suppose. I was just chatting with one of my coaching colleagues about this subject and recalled that I used to keep a diary when I was little. My family was very poor, and so I'd cut out pieces of used computer paper (my dad was a computer programmer) and make my own little books by stapling the pages together. Then I'd write about my day. I still have some of them stashed away in my mother's attic. They are full of misspellings and are written in block letters, as I hadn't learned how to write in cursive yet. My sisters were big readers, so I always thought that they were the smart ones and that I was the dumb one in the family. As I got older, my sisters both won spelling bee championships, and I never even tried to enter, since I was a terrible speller. Nevertheless, I was the one who always kept a journal, complete with all its misspellings. I still do. And funny enough, adopting the daily practice of writing is one of the best ways to write a book.

> *If children grew up according to early indications, we should have nothing but geniuses.*
>
> —JOHANN WOLFGANG VON GOETHE

I never thought that I could write well, because my father is an excellent writer and has written a novel; I knew I'd never be able to write the way he could. To compound matters, I was a slow reader as well as a rotten speller. In spite of that handicap, the English classes were my favorites, and after graduating from Georgetown's School of Foreign Service, I went on to get a master's in English at Georgetown (for fun). In one of those courses, the professor asked to see me in his office about the paper I had written. I was worried I had done something wrong. He told me my paper was excellent, gave me an A+ for it, and said it was worthy of submitting for publication. He offered to help me get it published, and I declined.

Looking back on it now, I can't believe I didn't say yes to his generous offer of support. Partly I didn't want to take his time, and partly I was just so convinced I wasn't a good writer that I couldn't imagine anyone's wanting to publish my paper. It wasn't until years later after reading a little book, *Simplify Your Life* by Elaine St. James, that it occurred to me to write a book about coaching. St. James's book is a short, square gift book containing one hundred tips on how to slow down and enjoy life—an excellent read, by the way. Each tip is about three paragraphs long. It inspired me to write a little tiny coaching book (at the time, there were no coaching books on the market) in the same style. I sat down and started to write and, over

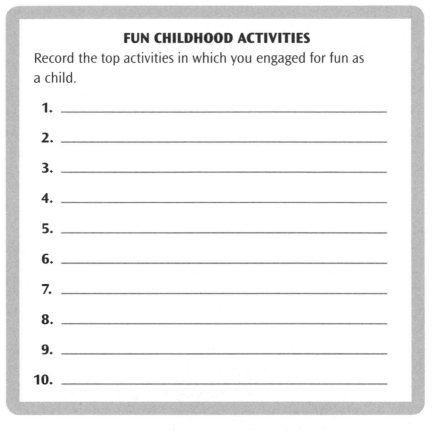

FUN CHILDHOOD ACTIVITIES

Record the top activities in which you engaged for fun as a child.

1. _____

2. _____

3. _____

4. _____

5. _____

6. _____

7. _____

8. _____

9. _____

10. _____

a period of about three months, wrote the whole thing. Then I sent it to Hyperion. They had published *Simplify Your Life*, so I thought, naively, that they would want to publish my book. They returned it with a form letter saying that they didn't accept unsolicited manuscripts. I could tell that a page hadn't even been turned.

I realized at that point that I might need an agent but didn't do anything at the time. It was a few months later that I received a call from an editor at Scribner who had read an article about me in *The Observer*, a local New York paper, and asked if I would write a book about coaching. When I said I already had, he nearly panicked until I explained that I was still working on the manuscript. He asked me to drop it off at his office and said he'd get back to me after he had a chance to read it. In the meantime, I was waiting with baited breath and wa[s sur]prised when he called me a few hours after I had deposite[d my] manuscript on his desk and enthusiastically told me, "You are a writer—your voice leaps right off the page!" It was then that I began to think that I could write. I was twenty-nine at that time, and my first book was *Coach Yourself to Success*, which went on to be published by Contemporary Books (now McGraw-Hill) and sell more than one hundred thousand copies around the world, was translated into seven foreign languages, and is still in print today ten years later. Not bad for the gal who can't spell

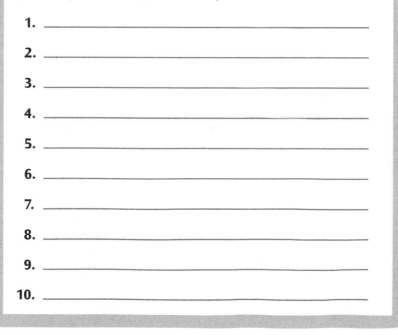

SUMMARY LIST OF STRENGTHS AND TALENTS

Now review everyone's feedback and create a full list of your strengths and innate talents. Is there a pattern? Does one thing keep coming up from a variety of people? Is there a thread that runs right through from childhood? That may be your unique talent or innate ability.

1. _____

2. _____

3. _____

4. _____

5. _____

6. _____

7. _____

8. _____

9. _____

10. _____

worth a darn! I'm not the first person to grow up in the shadow of a greater talent and assume that I'm not sufficiently talented in my own right.

Take some time to think of things you did as a child without any prompting. They may or may not be the source of a new career, but they will definitely lead to some activities you can do as an adult that recharge and energize you. There are home movies of me playing in the mud. If there was a mud puddle, I'd be sitting right in the middle of it as happy as can be. I even ate the mud. No surprise that I was drawn to pottery as an adult. It is one of the most relaxing and grounding hobbies I have tried. I love the feel of the clay between my fingers—always have. And some of my pieces were good enough that the shop owner sold them in her front window in New York City. So, hey, there may be a few pieces of "Talane-ware" out there yet. Who knows but I might just become a professional potter in my retirement.

One client said that she used to have a game she called "follow the cat"—she'd follow the family cat and let it lead her all over the house or the town. To this day she is lured by the unknown—not knowing what will happen or where things will go. She delights in exploring and having adventures. The adult version of this game is to book a holiday to a foreign country and explore the territory!

No one can be exactly like me. Sometimes even I have trouble doing it.

—TALLULAH BANKHEAD

Even if these assorted lists don't lead to a potential new career, they will lead to activities that give you loads of energy and are worth doing as hobbies for that reason alone. I've yet to come across someone who doesn't want more energy! Kids are full of energy because they are always doing things that give them energy. You can recapture the energy of your childhood by simply doing the adult version of your childhood pastimes. If you aren't sure of your direction, just experiment; you'll know you've found something that truly fits when you feel really great after doing it.

Signs You've Found Your Unique Talent

Here are some signs that you've found your unique talent:

→ It feels fun and easy.
→ You can do it for hours and are more energized, not less.
→ Time collapses around you—you lose track of the hours when you are engaged in your natural talent.
→ You create superior results with less effort.
→ You add value effortlessly to those around you.
→ It is easy to be successful.
→ You are happy and fulfilled.
→ You feel fully alive and self-expressed.

If you are still stuck like a fish in peanut butter, if work feels like a burden, if you feel that something is missing or that you haven't tapped into your full potential, then you have more discovery work to do! Once you seize on your unique gifts, life becomes unbelievably easy, a lot more fun, and much more rewarding financially and personally.

What's Your Personal Style?

Can you imagine life in the future and picture what your retirement will be like, or are you primarily focused on the present or short term? Do questions such as "Where do you see yourself in five years?" leave you mystified, or can you come up with some cogent answers?

Do you enjoy a conflict and maybe even start one or pick a fight on occasion, or do you shy away from conflict? Are you ambitious and driving, or do you prefer to take a backseat and let someone else lead the way? Do you prefer to be the boss and give the orders, or are you much more comfortable letting someone else set the direction?

Are you a "single-tasker" and apt to do your best work when you can focus on one project or element at a time? Or are you a multitasker and inclined to be bored silly if you don't have a few projects going on at once? Do you like a slow pace or a fast pace? Do you need a variety of activities to keep you from nodding off, or does having multiple demands just end up overwhelming you, with the result that you get nothing done?

> *Don't try to take on a new personality; it doesn't work.*
>
> —RICHARD M. NIXON

These are just a few of the questions to consider when you're defining the ideal career. It is no good being an introvert and taking a sales job in which you are expected to give presentations or entertain clients. You'll simply end up being exhausted all the time and wishing you could go home and read a good book. Likewise, if you are an extrovert, you'll find yourself moldering away in the back-office accounting department crunching numbers when you really need and want to be out talking and engaging with others. This point may sound blatantly obvious, but if you don't know yourself well, then it is easy to make a mistake and accept a job that will have you miserable and exhausted in no time flat.

We can adapt to just about anything for a short period, but if we are constantly in an environment that isn't suited to our natural style, we'll soon be exhausted, and if we persist, the condition can lead to sickness and disease. So, serious stuff not to be taken lightly!

I had one client, a journalist, who had been very happy in her work until the company reconfigured the entire office space to an open floor plan. No one had any privacy anymore, and the noise level soared. The idea behind the redesign was to encourage sharing of ideas and brainstorming. This arrangement may be stimulating for an extrovert, but it is sheer hell for an introvert. She noticed that her work was suffering, and she couldn't string two cogent sentences together. That was why she hired me; she thought she needed to find a different career. It didn't take long to figure out that all she needed was a bit of peace and quiet to allow her to write. She couldn't get that at the office, so I suggested she try working from home or grab her laptop and try working at a coffee shop. This move did the trick, and soon she was back in top form and back in her bosses' good graces. She had thought she was being a wimp and didn't realize that the work environment can make a huge difference in your performance, depending on your personal style.

Another client, a senior executive at a major U.S. bank, mentioned that she was worried about her new assistant. Ever since joining the company, her assistant just wasn't happy. I asked if I could give the assistant a few private coaching calls, and sure enough, we soon discovered that the assistant had been used to working in an office surrounded by a lot of other administrative assistants and executives. In the new office, she was on a separate floor all by herself. She was lonely and miserable, and it was a mental feat to get anything done. To make matters worse, with her boss now traveling more often, she didn't even have the person to whom she reported for company. Her friends and family told her that she should be happy to have some peace and quiet and gave her suggestions such as taking in a radio to keep her company, but these well-meaning comments didn't actually help. It reached the point that she had to take antidepressants to keep herself going. Good grief! I told her to make a strong request to move her desk to the floor with all the other people, and that was it. She is an extrovert and simply needs to be surrounded by people to keep from falling into a depression.

This is serious stuff. You can't adapt as much as you think you can without serious consequences to your performance, your health, and your happiness. This is why knowing what your personal style is can help you determine the best working environment. Having a document in black and white on an objective computerized report makes it easier for you to make the case with a boss or supervisor.

Different people have different styles, so some people may not appreciate that your needs are much different from theirs. We tend to think, "If I can do it, then so can you." This mind-set couldn't be further from the truth. While some individuals thrive on chaos and change, others thrive on stability and peace. Some do their best when they plan for the future and are hopeless with handling the day-to-day tasks. Others are best surrounded by people and need variety. As you read through the following five sections, take a few minutes to jot down your ratings in the spaces provided and identify your own personal style. For more detailed information about the computerized assessments, go to Lifecoach.com and get your own personalized report for a small fee, or consult the "Resources" section at the back of the book.

With a bit of thought, you can figure out your own personal style—the way in which you do things. Again, don't be afraid to ask a few people who know you well for their input. Here is a preview of the questions to get you thinking:

→ Are you an extrovert or an introvert?
→ Are you a tactical thinker or a strategic thinker?
→ Do you prefer to do one thing at a time or to multitask?
→ Are you hands-on or hands-off?
→ Are you quick to anger or slow to anger?

Extrovert Versus Introvert

Do you recharge your energy by being alone? Do you feel drained after being around people all day? If so, then you are more introverted than extroverted.

Do you feel energized by being around other people and become stimulated by external events? Do you feel drained or depressed after working alone all day and get the urge to go out and socialize? If so, then you are more extroverted and get your energy from contact with people and from outside activities and events.

Or, you may fall in the middle and need a good balance between being around others and time alone. If you are around people during the day, you may need to hole up at home and prefer not to go out in the evenings. If you can mix up the right balance between contact with people and time to yourself, you'll feel energized throughout the day.

Rate yourself (you'll be using a scale of 100 percent throughout) as to how much you are extroverted and how much you are introverted. We are all a combination of both, as even the most extroverted folks still need some time alone on occasion, and the most introverted need some contact with others. Then ask a close family member and friend to tell you how they would rate you on this scale as well, so you can see how others perceive you.

	MY RATING	FRIENDS, FAMILY, AND COWORKERS RATING
Extrovert	_____ %	_____ %
Introvert	_____ %	_____ %
Total =	**100%**	**100%**

Tactical Versus Strategic Thinker

Tactical thinkers are skillful at handling the present. They are excellent at getting tasks done quickly and efficiently, because they are short-term thinkers. They often have difficulty imagining where they will be in life in five years, let alone ten. They may be so focused on the present that they neglect planning for the future. Other people are strategic thinkers and can imagine what the future will hold and the impact their actions today will have over the passage of time. It depends on whether your brain is hardwired for the short term or the long term. Certain people are good midrange planners and think five years or so into the future. If you are a long-term thinker, then you may also tend to procrastinate. This is because you feel there is always more time.

Both sides of the spectrum come with pros and cons. The short-term thinkers may not think about saving for their retirement, while the long-term thinker may be putting things off today—why rush when there is plenty of time? This is why some people are proficient at tactical or short-term planning but hopeless when asked to think about where they will be in ten or twenty years.

My husband is a tactical thinker and is brilliant at dispatching tasks, whereas I think approximately twenty years into the future and tend to put off the daily duties. When I met him, he didn't have any retirement savings at all. As a team, we balance each other out, although I can drive him crazy going on about possible scenarios in the future, to which he comes back at me with, "Let's just get this handled for the present and worry about the future later." Typical for someone with a time frame of six months!

Again, take a few minutes to think about where you fall on this spectrum. (Tactical: Zero- to five-year time frame. Strategic: Five- to ten-plus-year time frame.) If you are in the middle, you can imagine the impact of your actions about one to five years out.

	MY RATING	FRIENDS, FAMILY, AND COWORKERS RATING
Tactical	_____ %	_____ %
Strategic	_____ %	_____ %
Total =	**100%**	**100%**

One Thing at a Time Versus Multitasking

Almost all of my clients think that they are multitaskers—that they thrive on having a number of things to do at once. This tendency may be a result of living in a multitasking world. We often have to multitask, so we end up doing it, but that doesn't mean it is actually our natural or preferred style. In fact, according to *The Universal Language DISC* by Bill Bonnstetter and his team at Target Training International, at least 50 percent of us are single-taskers and do our best work and are most productive when we allow ourselves to focus on one thing at a time. The single-taskers also tend to do their best work in a slower-paced environment. If too much is going on at once, they are overwhelmed and become inefficient. The fast-paced work environment typically appeals to the multitaskers, who thrive on a bit of chaos and commotion.

Try this experiment and see whether you are a natural single-tasker: Clean off everything from your desk, divert the phones, and turn off the e-mail message reminder. Tell associates that you can't be disturbed for the next hour or two. Now work on just *one* thing, and give yourself permission to do that and only that. . . . How did it go? Did you get an impressive amount accomplished in a relatively short period? Did you feel thoroughly satisfied with your achievement? If you sometimes feel you'd like the world to stop, you are in all probability a single-tasker. If, on the other hand, you struggled to focus and wanted to break up this task with other tasks, then you are a multitasker by nature and would perform better by having two or three projects going simultaneously.

Some of my clients have two or three desks or workstations in their offices and have a different project in process on each sur-face. To stay motivated, they move from station to station to work on these various projects whenever they feel their enthusiasm or energy waning. This setup keeps them happy, and they get more accomplished than they would if they had to do one project at a time, which they find too boring. Experiment and you'll soon dis cover your natural style

For single-taskers, heaven is being given just one thing to do and the uninterrupted time in which to complete it. When some-one suggested that I pack up my bags and go on an authors' retreat at a B and B to work on this book, I nearly salivated. Nothing to do but write? No business matters to attend to, e-mails to answer, or kids to look after? That would be wonderful—for a week. It also feeds the extrovert in me, as I could hang out with the other writers after putting in a good day at the keyboard or sneak out for lunch or for a break. Pure heaven! Most people don't have the luxury of working on one thing at a time, especially if their bosses ask them to take on multiple projects, but at least give yourself the illusion of doing so by putting just a sole project on your desk at any one time. You'll stand to be much more productive if you work with your natural style and not against it.

	MY RATING	FRIENDS, FAMILY, AND COWORKERS RATING
Single-tasker	_____ %	_____ %
Multitasker	_____ %	_____ %
Total =	**100%**	**100%**

Hands-On (Practical) Versus Hands-Off (Abstract)

Some people have the need to work with their hands and produce a tangible product or result, while others are content to work in the abstract and don't need to put their hands on an object to feel that they've accomplished something. As more and more jobs become abstract and require dealing with people, concepts, and ideas, often the only physical evidence of a hard day's work is a printed report or memo. As jobs become increasingly abstract, people with the need to produce something tangible may feel vaguely or even highly dissatisfied with their work.

People who are hands-off like the abstract and don't need a physical product or result to feel satisfaction with their work. They may be perfectly content to let others do the actual physical work and have no inclination to get their hands dirty. The hands-on folks are the ones who get a real sense of satisfaction from building something or creating something with their hands and need this level of involvement to feel they are getting something done. One of the most common causes of dissatisfaction—and it often comes at about age forty—is a job that entails doing abstract work. If you come home after a day's work and feel as if you haven't accomplished anything real, even though you did in fact get a lot done, this may be a sign that you need to do something with your hands.

If your work doesn't have scope for this type of activity, take up a hobby such as pottery, gardening, or woodworking—anything that would enable you to create a tangible and concrete result. You may find that this outlet is all you need to eliminate that vague discontent. After we reach the age of forty, typically our need to express our hands-on side becomes even stronger. This phenomenon may even be what people often think of as a midlife crisis.

Common examples of occupations that suit this hands-on desire are bricklayers, carpenters, mechanics, surgeons, chefs, physical therapists, musicians, dentists, chiropractors, painters, and decorators. Included among abstract professions are teachers, coaches, executives, managers, and salespeople, who primarily deal with ideas, concepts, and people, as opposed to things or products.

	MY RATING	FRIENDS, FAMILY, AND COWORKERS RATING
Hands-off	_____ %	_____ %
Hands-on	_____ %	_____ %
Total =	**100%**	**100%**

Quick to Anger (Hot-Tempered) Versus Slow to Anger (Hold a Grudge)

If you are quick to anger, but then just as quickly let it blow over, you are probably among the 11 percent of the population who are born to lead according to *The Universal Language DISC*. You make decisions expeditiously and aren't afraid of a conflict. You may even create a conflict just because you rather enjoy duking it out verbally with someone. On the other hand, if you try to avoid conflict at all costs, you are like most people and are usually much slower to anger but may end up holding a secret grudge for years and never saying anything about it. You may have difficulty coming to a prompt decision and need time to consider all the alternatives.

Those who are decisive, strong-willed, and ambitious tend to end up in positions of leadership in corporations or to run their own businesses. They have a sense of urgency, aren't afraid of much, and can prod others into action. A tip for those of us who are a bit afraid of these types: stand up to them and don't be afraid to go head-to-head in an argument. They will respect you and won't think negatively of you if you assert your opinions. Just keep it brief and to the point; be prepared, and don't ramble on.

	MY RATING	FRIENDS, FAMILY, AND COWORKERS RATING
Quick to anger	_____ %	_____ %
Slow to anger	_____ %	_____ %
Total =	**100%**	**100%**

How to Make Your Natural Talents and Personal Style Work for You

The categories addressed in this chapter are just a few of the areas that you will want to take into consideration when looking for a new career. There is no getting around the fact that if you are born to lead, you won't last long in a subservient position with no chance for advancement or promotion. You'll soon blow up and say something inappropriate and then either get fired or quit. By the same token, if you need peace and quiet to work, you'll be miserable in a loud, chaotic workplace. Yes, we can all adapt for a certain period, but the longer you work in an environment that isn't suited to your natural style, the more miserable and stressed you'll become. Sometimes the problem isn't that you are in the wrong job, but rather it is that you are in the wrong environment.

Managers, take note: the fact that you thrive on one style doesn't mean your staff works the same way. You'll get the best out of your team by leveraging people's individual styles. That may mean you give Joe a single project to focus on while Jane gets three at once. The extroverts may respond well to the open floor plan, but make sure you have some quiet office spaces far from the crowd in which introverts can hunker down. Why not try something really radical and ask your employees what they need to do their best work and then provide that?

The simple exercises you completed are a remarkably good way to get some insight into your unique talents and abilities, but that effort may not be sufficient for everyone. If you feel satisfied that you've found your talent or natural gift, that's super. Pursue it with everything you've got. If not or if you are still a bit unsure or hesitant, you may want to consider taking some computerized assessments such as the StrengthsFinder Profile and/or The Highlands Program. Seeing the results confirmed in black and white on an objective, computerized report often helps us realize that we aren't just kidding ourselves and that yes, we do have a real ability that is worth investing time, money, and energy in developing. I always recommend that my clients take these online assessments before investing thousands of dollars and years of time in advanced training and education.

I was recently working with a young woman who had postponed going to a university because she wasn't sure what she should study. We did The Highlands Program and in two and a half hours confirmed that she does indeed have a natural and strong ability in artistic and creative design. She confessed that she loved design work and had thoroughly enjoyed doing layouts and artwork but wasn't sure that she was good enough to pursue it or that she could make a decent living. I reminded her that Andy Warhol was an extremely successful artist and assured her that even if she wasn't a famous artist, she could still make a good living doing creative work such as Web design, graphic design, or magazine layouts—doing something she truly loved. Seeing her assessment results spelled out on paper made her realize that her talent wasn't a fantasy. This realization has given her the confidence to pursue what she secretly wanted to do all along—art!

She has signed up for a foundation course in the arts so she can experience a variety of media and determine her specialty in time. Her parents couldn't believe the difference it made in their daughter and thanked me for my part in the transformation. See the Resources section in the back of the book for more information on these valuable computerized assessments.

With your natural talents and personal style identified, you are poised to find the career that puts those talents and abilities to use. This is one of the most important elements of finding the ideal career, so make sure you spend some time investigating your inherent abilities as opposed to your learned skills. Once you know what your special gifts are, the next step is to start orienting your entire life around the expression of those gifts and talents.

Identify Your Passions and Values

With definite goals you release your own power, and things start happening.

—ZIG ZIGLAR

The ideal combination is to find a natural talent or ability that is also a match to your passions, values, and interests. In practice, this doesn't always work out so neatly. You may have an absolute passion for golf, but if you aren't a natural athlete, then you may need to consider golf a fun hobby and not a serious profession. Alternatively, if your brain is wired to do higher mathematics, but you aren't interested in math, you probably aren't going to sign up for that advanced calculus class. Whatever the circumstances, I would certainly encourage a client to pursue any of his or her top ten abilities, because often once we try something that is one of our natural talents (even if we didn't know it at the time), it ends up being a rewarding and successful career. The process is fairly obvious: if we have a natural talent, then with a bit of study and practice, we can become masterful relatively quickly. And mastery is often rewarding financially as well as personally. No mystery there.

> *Choose a job you love and you'll never have to work a day in your life.*
>
> —CONFUCIUS

The big problem is that most people aren't aware of their own natural talents and abilities or even of their core values. I had no idea that coaching was one of my natural talents. I was working in the bank, and although I easily developed relationships with my clients, I certainly wasn't coaching them to have a better life. I was limited to helping them sort out their financial lives or choose the best loan product. With a certain amount of skepticism, I signed up for professional coaching classes and started working with my first clients while still working at the bank. Being a coach was so much fun and so easy that it has never felt like work. Before I had finished the curriculum, I was teaching coaching skills to the other students at Coach U. In contrast, after a day at the bank I'd come home drained. I'd collapse on the sofa and take a short nap, and then I'd get up and start coaching clients. By the time I had finished coaching at ten P.M., I was so energized that I'd have trouble getting to sleep. Most people experience the same effect. When we are doing something we are hardwired to do—an innate talent—and it is in alignment with one of our top values, not only can we quickly become masterful, but also we get naturally energized from the task.

Conversely, when you do something for which you aren't naturally built, your energy can drain away. That doesn't mean you won't do a good job. If you are smart enough or work hard enough, you can learn to do all sorts of things and do them well. Just prepare yourself for the fact that it may take more time, energy, and practice for you than the next person. One client holds three advanced degrees but has always had difficulty remembering what she has read. When asked how she succeeded academically, she admitted that when everyone else was out sharing a pizza on a Friday night, she'd be home reading the textbook for a third time. Our passions and interests can make up for a lack of natural ability. On the other hand, it is less likely that you'll encounter a top musician who doesn't have raw musical talent, because the field is so competitive that those without the talent are soon overtaken by those with that inherent ability. Although, Madonna is an excellent example of a singer who didn't have much natural talent to start but over the years has significantly improved her singing voice. So, don't let a lack of natural talent stop you if you have the passion!

There are two types of values related to this topic. The first type are often subconscious; we aren't actually aware of how they influence and affect our daily lives. I call these our hidden motivators. These are the values that determine the choices we make in life: what cars we drive, why we pursue a certain career over another, how we spend our money, and so on. The second type are the core values, and those are simply the things that we love to do—our passions. These are often, but not always, more obvious. For example, you may be fully aware that you are passionate about fine wines, traveling, or stamp collecting but may not be aware of the particular core value behind these different activities. Once you identify that core value, it is easier to discover other activities and careers that will make you happy, because you understand the underlying value. Let's start by examining your hidden motivation.

The Six Hidden Motivators

Knowing why you make the choices you do is also very helpful in choosing the correct career. There are six core driving values that influence your everyday choices in life, from your type of transportation to whether you'd paint a wall in your house:

Money/practicality
Power/influence over others
Beauty/harmony
Service to others
System for living/principles
Knowledge/truth

> *A great many people have asked how I manage to get so much work done and still keep looking so dissipated.*
>
> —ROBERT BENCHLEY

Remember that knowledge of these drivers will help you realize your true passions and values and, in turn, will help you in your search for a rewarding career or job transition. Let's explore these drivers in more detail.

Money/Practicality

A practical person is one who, when considering an option, asks him- or herself the question, "How is this useful?" Practical people will work hard to make a good living and provide for their dependents. Money is important to them, and they often are good businesspeople who

> *Money is better than poverty, if only for financial reasons.*
>
> —WOODY ALLEN

excel at setting and achieving goals. Money may also be a scorecard for them, and they are motivated to work hard if they know there is a financial reward. They may also foster relationships with people who can be useful or helpful to them in the future. Their orientation to life is practical.

Power/Influence over Others

The person who works hard to be the boss, leader, or manager and likes to have influence or control over others is motivated by the desire for power. Such people may become involved in politics or seek similar positions of power, control, influence, and leadership, whether that is to head a company, serve as the pastor of a church, or preside over the PTA.

> *I am the state.*
>
> —LOUIS XIV

Beauty/Harmony

If beauty and harmony motivate you, you may find that you can't work or live in a place that isn't beautiful. You make an effort to live in a beautiful place and see the beauty in all things. You are motivated to become the best person you can be and deem personal growth and development important. Your life itself may be like a work of art. One need not be an artist or a creative person to value beauty and harmony.

Service to Others

If you would give the shirt off your back to help another, then you are motivated by service. You are naturally selfless and give to others even at your own expense. You may consider people who are motivated by some of the other values to be cold or self-serving.

People in this category include the social workers, the caretakers, the assistants, the full-time parents, the nurses and doctors, and the Mother Teresas of the world. If your primary goal in life is to help or serve others, then service is your motivating value.

System for Living/Principles

As Ralph Waldo Trine said, "There are many who are living far below their possibilities because they are continually handing over their individualities to others. Do you want to be a power in the world? Then be yourself. Be true to the highest within your soul and then allow yourself to be governed by no customs or conventionalities or arbitrary man-made rules that are not founded on principle." This pretty much sums up the belief of the highly principled. If you would die before sacrificing your principles, or if you have a structured or rigid system for living, then this is one of your hidden drivers. For some people, it takes the form of a religion, which they use as a doctrine or code to live by. Or it may be that you are an environmentalist, a yogi, or a vegan, and this practice informs the choices you make about how to live.

People who are highly principled will fight for their beliefs and may dedicate their lives to spreading the word. Gandhi is among the most famous exemplars. A missionary who goes into dangerous or disease-ridden areas to convert the natives would have to be strongly principled to risk his or her life for this purpose. On a more mundane level, you may just be the "green" one who recycles everything and can't help but look down on those who don't. There is a

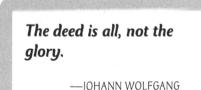

The deed is all, not the glory.

—JOHANN WOLFGANG VON GOETHE

tendency among those motivated by their principles to be judgmental of those who don't follow suit. They sincerely believe that if everyone were to do adopt their chosen system, the world would be a better place.

Knowledge/Truth

This category applies if you are motivated by discovering the truth and gaining knowledge. In order to feel satisfied in your work, you need to have an intellectual challenge. A job loses your interest when you've learned all you can there; you need a bigger intellectual challenge. Einstein is a familiar example of dedicating one's life to the quest for knowledge and truth. Research scientists, academics, teachers, professors, writers, and journalists all may have knowledge as a motivating value. Because people of this type are motivated by learning, they may take a job that pays less than they could make elsewhere if it is mentally challenging or stimulating. If this is your motivating value, you probably have a hard time getting out of a bookstore.

> *Rather than love, than money, than fame, give me truth.*
>
> —HENRY DAVID THOREAU

Identify Your Own Hidden Motivators

Review the preceding list of the six hidden motivators and choose the two that are the strongest for you, then the two that may apply some of the time but not always, and finally the two about which you are indifferent. Among my clients, this is how people typically rank their values: in pairs, from most important to least important. Occasionally, however, I meet someone who has three strong motivating values instead of two.

The kind of car you drive or would choose to drive may be a good indicator of your values. One client drives a beautiful old Jaguar. Every other week it is in the shop for one reason or another. He doesn't care. He cherishes his car. His primary value is *beauty*, and he doesn't mind that the car doesn't actually function that well as a car. He marvels over its clean lines and luxurious leather interior. Whether it actually functions reliably as a car isn't as important. He is indifferent about money and practicality.

Another client, Rachel, always has the latest clothes and fashions. On the surface one might guess she values beauty, but her hidden motivators are *power* and *money*. She wears the lovely clothes to get ahead in her career and project the image of success. If you were to follow her actions, you'd learn that all her clothes are bought at discount or sample sales. (Bargain hunters often value money above the other drivers and will spend time to find the object they want for the best possible price.) She is in sales, a career well suited to her values, as she works diligently to bring in the deal and is motivated to earn the commission. Most people, as surprising as it may seem, have the beauty and harmony motivator on the bottom of the list.

> *Ours is a world where people don't know what they want and are willing to go through hell to get it.*
>
> —DON MARQUIS

Then there is Janet, who is selfless and, naturally enough, is a social worker. While she makes only a modest amount of money, she is happy to be helping people who are in need. She knows she is making a difference, and that is most important to her. She is devoted to *serving and helping others*, and although she wishes the job paid more, money isn't as important to her.

The yogi who practices meditation and eats a vegetarian diet is strongly *principled*. He has a rigid and structured system for living, with rules that apply to the time he goes to bed at night, what sort of foods to eat during the day, what service to engage in, and how long to meditate. The yogi who actually runs the ashram may be highly principled and, at the same time, have the motivator of power or influence over others, even though he exercises this influence in a gentle and soft-spoken manner.

The person who could happily and easily spend a few hours hanging out at the bookstore and often has loads of books at home probably values truth and knowledge. You might be curious and simply want to know things even if they do not have any practical application to your life. The quest for truth and knowledge may not seem sensible to those around you with different values. The more practical person might say, "Why do you want to learn about that? I don't see the point." The point is simply the acquisition of more knowledge. This person will require a job that challenges his or her knowledge and provides the opportunity to learn new things in order to feel satisfied at work.

Another client, as I noted earlier, had three top values: power, money, and service. He was an entrepreneur, so he could run the show (power), and he was brilliant at making money, but he wasn't satisfied if his business didn't help others, so he set it up to direct a percentage of the profits to his favorite charity.

Give some thought to your hidden or not-so-hidden motivating values. What informs your choices in life? When couples fight, or when we can't understand why someone would make that "ridiculous" choice, it is often because the parties involved hold different values. If you think it is nuts to own a car that is always in the shop, you probably value practicality more than beauty. If you are reluctant to spend money on the finer things in life, again, that practical nature holds sway. If you spend time poring over magazines devoted to fashion or decorating or would buy a gorgeous pair of shoes even though you really should buy a new toaster, beauty may be your thing. If you always prefer to be the one in charge, then power may be one of your top values. If you spend a ton of money every month on books, or if you play bridge or chess for fun in your spare time, then knowledge may be your leading value. If you spend time helping others, then service may be one of your main values.

It helps to think about what is really important to you in life. Doing so makes it easier to make the right choices. The chiropractor I mentioned earlier in Step 3, who wasn't sure whether to grow his practice or shrink it, just needed to take stock of his motivating values. He valued beauty and knowledge. In his spare time he'd read books on the top of a mountain. Not expensive habits or hobbies. The irony is that even though money and power were not his values, his practice was actually more profitable when he reduced it in size, as he reduced his overhead as well.

If it still isn't clear to you which of these are your top ones (and that isn't unusual, as our underlying values have so much bearing on the way we see the world that sometimes it is hard to recognize what they are, because we assume everyone sees things from the same perspective), please consult the Resources section in the back of the book for information on taking a computerized assessment called The Career Planning Insights Report and Workplace Motivators Report that will reveal your top motivating values in ten minutes.

Identify Your Core Values

You've identified your hidden motivators, so let's proceed to take a look at your core values—the things that are most important to you and that you love to do. It doesn't take an Einstein to figure out that if you love what you do, you'll be more inclined to do it to the point of reaching mastery. Look at Bill Gates as an example. It appears that he was born a computer whiz, but it takes more than natural ability to become successful. He was lucky to have been exposed to the big mainframe computers when he was a kid, but that exposure wasn't enough; he clearly had a passion for computers. He used to get up in the middle of the

> *Try not to become a man of success, but rather try to become a man of value.*
>
> —ALBERT EINSTEIN

night and sneak out of the house without waking his parents in order to go to the local library, where he could use the computers for free from two A.M. to six A.M. His mother didn't realize until he confessed years later why he was so tired during the day. If you want to find work that you'll still love years down the road, then you'll definitely want to make sure that it matches at least one of your top values and passions. The more of your core values that you can express through your work, the happier you'll be, and the longer you'll be satisfied in your career.

While most of my clients have resisted doing the personal and emotional requirements analyses, they all enjoy the values work, because we treasure our values. Values give our lives meaning, joy, and happiness. Our values and peak experiences are the source of profound fulfillment, passion, bliss, and even euphoria—all of which are components to finding the right career. If you have taken the time to identify and fulfill your personal requirements in Step 2 and yet you aren't happy in your current career, then it is high time that you start living your values; the source of excitement, joy, and a sense of fulfillment and of living your purpose all come from expressing your core values. Especially if you want to attract the right career to you, start living your values today. More opportunities arise when we are doing what we love to do.

What makes you feel turned on and excited about life? What are your passions? What has you bouncing out of bed in the morning, eager to start the day? These are our core values, and when we are living them regularly, we feel excited about life; we radiate energy and enthusiasm. You are most likely to attract the ideal career when you are fully living and expressing your core values. If you keep hitting the snooze button every morning or need multiple cups of coffee to motivate yourself to start the day, you aren't doing what you love to do. When we love our work and our lives, we are naturally motivated to perform our duties. You won't need artificial stimuli to get out of bed and get started. If you do not have a highly satisfying life now and are waiting for the right career or the big promotion to land on your lap, think again. You are responsible for your own happiness and success. The best way to attract a desirable career opportunity is to not need one (hence the Personal Requirements Quiz and exercises in Step 2) and to

> *Success is not the result of spontaneous combustion. You must set yourself on fire.*
>
> —REGGIE LEACH

be living the best possible life you can right now (the passions and values work). One of the easiest ways to figure out what you secretly want so badly that you can taste it is to examine your envy.

The Envy Method

Envy is one of the seven deadly sins, but I actually find it a useful tool for discovering people's deeper desires, dreams, and values. As a matter of fact, it is such a good method that if I had only five minutes to coach you to find the ideal career, I would simply ask you to name someone you envy and explain why. Envy precisely reveals what you secretly wish you could have or be. What you envy in others is what you want for yourself but, for some perverse reason, don't think you can have. Whose career do you envy? Is the source of your envy something the person has, is it a certain quality or characteristic, or is it a particular achievement? In what ways do you want to be like this person, have what this person has, or do what he or she is doing? How you respond to these questions is an excellent indication of your own passions and values. If you are in awe of what somebody else possesses or has achieved in his or her walk of life, then this is what you want for yourself. If you thought you could have it, you wouldn't be feeling envious; you'd be feeling inspired to change your career path and try something new.

> *Regret for the things we did can be tempered by time; it is regret for the things we did not do that is inconsolable.*
>
> —SYDNEY J. HARRIS

I was working with a client to help her figure out what she wanted to do with her career. She had been an extremely successful commercial real-estate developer in the United States until she married and moved abroad and was left at loose ends. She considered doing real estate again but felt she had already been there and done that. I ran her through a battery of computerized assessments to see what her innate abilities were, and then I simply asked her to tell me about someone she envied. She admitted, rather sheepishly, to envying Diane von Furstenburg, the fashion designer. Guess what: she secretly wanted to become a designer herself but never thought she could be successful at it. I took a look at her strengths and abilities and pointed out that there was no reason whatsoever why she couldn't be successful in this field. She had everything it would take and just needed to get started. She even had a handy list of close friends in the field she could consult for advice and information. Why we have this perverse notion that we can't do what those we envy do is a mystery to me, because more often than not, you can! What's more, the person you envy proved that it's possible!

> *It is not irritating to be where one is. It is only irritating to think one would like to be somewhere else.*
>
> —JOHN CAGE

Make a list of all the people you envy and what specifically you want that they have, using the space provided in this section. Also consider those you admire and what it is you admire about them. We often admire others for what we want to be, do, or have as well. However, admiration isn't quite as effective a guide as envy for discovering your real desires and passions in life. We may admire qualities or abilities in another that we don't actually want for ourselves. For example, you may admire Venus Williams's ability with the tennis racket but may have no interest in playing tennis yourself. You may, however, envy her lifestyle or fame because you secretly want that yourself. Envy is a bad thing only when you think you can't have the object of your envy. Again, the fact that one person has achieved it proves that it is humanly possible to do and paves the way forward for you. No need to reinvent the wheel; just reinvent

> *My motto is "Contented with little, yet wishing for more."*
>
> —CHARLES LAMB

yourself. Use the envy method to figure out what you really want. Works every time! It is one of the surest and best indicators for figuring out what path to take in your career and life.

When you are green with envy, that is the green light to go for it! Then you'll discover that your envy suddenly morphs into inspiration. Following is a sample "Envy" list:

PEOPLE I ENVY	WHAT I WANT THAT THEY HAVE
1. Oprah Winfrey	Great wealth and ability to influence others
2. Bill Clinton	Charisma
3. Dalai Lama	Peace/awareness/spirituality
4. Coaching colleague	Bestselling author/fame
5. Tony Robbins	Getting well compensated for a keynote speech
6. Seminar leader	Ability to change someone's life with a conversation

Now make your own list:

PEOPLE I ENVY	WHAT I WANT THAT THEY HAVE
1. _____	_____
2. _____	_____
3. _____	_____
4. _____	_____
5. _____	_____
6. _____	_____
7. _____	_____
8. _____	_____
9. _____	_____
10. _____	_____

The Core Values and Passions List

Another way to discover your values and passions is by simply studying a list of the most common ones and seeing what pops out that you most want to do. Review the extensive list that follows, and circle the words that strike you as something you'd love your life to be about. If you'd bounce out of bed in the morning to be involved in it, that is a good indication it is a core value. You can circle the heading or subheadings—it doesn't matter; just select as many values as appeal to you. If you weren't worried about money or status and you could wake up and do what you most desired, what would it be? Imagine that money is no object. Remember that this is not the time to be practical or realistic. Just pick what makes your heart sing. If you hold a value that is not provided on the list, feel free to add it.

The list entries are mostly verbs or other action-oriented words. These are the things we most want to do in life. Some people find that there is some overlap with their list of top four needs from the Personal Requirements Quiz in Step 2. The difference between a need and a value or passion is that you *must* fulfill your needs or else there will be a negative consequence or reaction. For example, if you don't win, you may get crabby or irritable. However, if to win is one of your values, that means that you would love your life to be about winning or would prefer to win on a regular basis, but if you don't win, it isn't the end of the world and you would be a good sport about it. Conversely, if you have the need to win, you may find it very difficult to be a gracious loser and may even storm out of the room in anger if you lose a card or board game.

In other words, our personal requirements are what we *need* to be our best, whereas our core values are about ultimate fulfillment in work and life—that is the state when we feel we are fulfilling our destiny and living our purpose, when we are excited about our work and are naturally motivated and energized. When our careers are an expression of our core values, we are naturally excited about life, and we eagerly embrace any work there is to do. While fulfilling our personal requirements creates a sense of satisfaction and contentment, fulfilling our core values leads to euphoria, bliss, happiness, and joy.

As you read through the Core Values and Passions that follow, it is OK to circle numerous entries; you can narrow your selections afterward. Pick what you are naturally drawn to, what excites or interests you, and not what you think you should do to be successful. Do not trouble yourself now about how you'll make money doing something that sounds like so much fun. We'll focus on that later. Just pick the values and passions that you most want your career and life to be about.

CORE VALUES AND PASSIONS

→ **Adventure.** Traveling to foreign countries; exploring the unknown; camping; meeting new people; taking big risks; starting your own business; betting or gambling; playing poker or similar card games; engaging in physically dangerous or challenging activities such as bungee jumping, skydiving, mountain climbing, rappelling, ice camping, and scuba diving

Challenge	Chance	Danger	Dare
Endeavor	Enterprise	Exhilaration	Experiment
Explore	Gamble	Hazard	Journey
Pioneer	Quest	Risk	Roam
Speculate	Thrill	Travel	The unknown
Venture	Wager	Wander	

→ **Seeking beauty.** Spending time in nature; visiting art exhibits, galleries, and museums; decorating your home; antique hunting; designing a beautiful wardrobe; looking as attractive as possible; listening to music; going to concerts; living in a beautiful location; eating at the best restaurants; surrounding yourself with luxury; renovating a home; making something beautiful; being a stylist, hairdresser, artist, sculptor, painter, or musician

Artistic	Attractive	Beautify	Civilize
Cultivate	Culture	Decorate	Elaborate
Elegance	Embellish	Enhance	Freshen
Gloriousness	Improve	Loveliness	Magnificence
Nature	Perfect	Polish	Radiance
Refine	Reform	Renovate	Taste
Transform			

→ **Catalyze.** Coaching; mentoring; speaking; writing; persuading; leading; lobbying; managing a team; encouraging others to move forward in any way; tutoring; volunteering

Alter	Animate	Arouse	Coach
Encourage	Energize	Excite	Exhilarate
Exhort	Galvanize	Impact	Impassion
Impel	Incite	Influence	Instigate
Lobby	Motivate	Move	Persuade
Prompt	Spark	Spur	Stimulate
Touch	Transform	Turn on	Urge

→ **Contribute.** Volunteering for a charity; tutoring children or adults; visiting or caring for disabled, sick, or elderly people; helping others; being a minister or volunteering for a church or a community service; coaching; mentoring; helping others grow or develop

Administer	Advance	Aid	Assist
Augment	Bestow	Donate	Endow
Facilitate	Foster	Give	Grant
Help	Impart	Improve	Invest
Minister to	Offer	Provide	Serve
Share	Strengthen	Support	Tithe

→ **Create.** Inventing a product or service; writing articles or books; designing anything, such as being an architect, interior designer, composer, chef, jewelry maker, fashion designer, floral designer, furniture maker, builder, craftsperson, sculptor, artist, musician, screenplay writer, film director, or producer; taking art, drawing, writing, or pottery classes

Assemble	Birth	Build	Compose
Conceive	Concoct	Construct	Craft
Create	Design	Develop	Devise
Dream	Evolve	Fabricate	Generate
Imagine	Ingenuity	Initiate	Innovate
Inspire	Invent	Make	Originate
Perfect	Plan	Start	Synthesize
Think			

→ **Discover.** Working as a detective or an investigator; learning new things; reading books; taking adult education courses or personal development courses; being a scientist, researcher, or analyst; reading nonfiction books to expand your knowledge

Absorb	Ascertain	Behold	Bring to light
Contemplate	Detect	Discern	Distinguish
Examine	Find	Gain	Investigate
Knowledge	Learn	Locate	Observe
Penetrate	Perceive	Read	Realize
Spy	Study	Uncover	Watch

→ **Feel.** Instructing dance; doing yoga, meditating; practicing tai chi; learning to give Reiki or massage; taking any experiential course or learning a profession involving activities such as healing, Reiki, or massage; working in the intuitive, sensing, or sensory fields, such as being a chef, taster, or perfumer

Awareness	Be in touch with	Be with	Dance
Emote	Experience	Feel good	Glow
Hear	Intuit	Notice	Perceive
Scent	Sense	sensations	Touch
Vibrate	Taste		

→ **Lead.** Leading a team, company, or expedition; being a role model; taking on leadership roles in the community or church; being a manager or boss; being a public speaker; being the leader of a cause or movement; being a leader in your field or hobby; influencing or persuading others to adopt your point of view

Be the chief	Cause	Direct	Dominate
Encourage	Enroll	Forge ahead	Govern
Guide	Head	Influence	Inspire
Lead	Manage	Model	Order
Persuade	Pioneer	Reign	Rule

→ **Master.** Being a master or an expert in your field or hobby; taking courses to refine and develop your natural strengths; reaching the pinnacle of your vocation or craft; being a master woodworker, artisan, actor, singer, bond trader, teacher, or doctor; continually striving to be the best; honing your skills; seeking ongoing training, education, or coaching

Adept	Be the best	Champion	Competence
Conquer	Deft	Dexterous	Dominate field
Excel	Experience	Expert	Genius
Greatest	Know-how	Outdo	Preeminence
Primacy	Proficient	Prowess	Skill
Superiority	Superstar	Talent	Understanding
Wisdom			

→ **Play.** Having fun; going to the movies; shopping; dancing; painting; reading for pleasure; eating in fine restaurants; having great sex; playing games or sports; playing card or board games; going to the theater or concerts; going to parties; entertaining others; taking a course for fun or pleasure; going to a comedy show; going camping; having a picnic; taking a scenic drive

Amuse oneself	Be amused	Be entertained	Be hedonistic
Be merry	Be sensual	Caper	Carefree

Comedy	Dance	Dining	Enjoyment
Frolic	Have fun	Joke	Laugh
Play games	Revel	Rollick	Sensuality
Sports			

→ **Relate/communicate.** Holding a family reunion; setting up a family website to keep in contact, post photos, and chat online; joining a group in your community; joining or starting a book club; having family dinners; having friends and/or family over for potluck suppers

Affiliate	Associate	Be in touch	Be part of community
Be with	Belong	Bond	Communicate
family/friends	Converse	Forge	Integrate
Connect	Join	Link	Speak
Involve	Unite		
Talk			

→ **Be sensitive.** Being a healer, massage therapist, counselor, or coach; visiting homes for children with special needs, senior citizens, or people with disabilities; volunteering or working for soup kitchens or charities; volunteering or working on a support phone line; volunteering to hold babies in hospitals

Be affected	Be compassionate	Be moved	Be present
Be tender	Care	Emote	Empathize
Feel	Melt	Perceive	Respond
See	Soften	Support	Sympathize
Take to heart	Touch one's heart		

→ **Be spiritual.** Joining a church, religious, or spiritual group; meditating; keeping a journal; being a yoga teacher or doing yoga; being a nun, monk, minister, rabbi, priest, or spiritual leader

Be accepting	Be awake	Be aware	Be passionate
Blessed	Canonized	Deify	Devoted

Devout	Glorify	Grace	Honor
Meditate	Piety	Practice a religion	Practice holiness
Pray	Purify	Relate with God	Sacredness
Sainted	Sanctify	Theist	Zealot

→ **Teach.** Being a teacher, trainer, lecturer, or public speaker; hosting a radio show; teaching English in a foreign country; being an adjunct professor in your area of expertise at a local college or university; tutoring children or adults; teaching adult education classes; coaching

Advise	Civilize	Coach	Consult
Cultivate	Demonstrate	Direct	Edify
Educate	Enlighten	Explain	Expound
Give lessons	Guide	Illuminate	Improve
Indoctrinate	Inform	Instruct	Lecture
Mentor	Preach	Prepare	Prime
School	Sermonize	Show	Train
Tutor	Uplift		

→ **Win.** Regularly engaging in sports or games that you are likely to win; hosting a weekly card party; setting goals and objectives so that you can win in your life; working with a coach or trainer to gain the edge over competition

Accomplish	Acquire	Attain	Attract
Be first	Be victorious	Conquer	Gain
Predominate	Prevail	Score	Triumph
Win over			

Do not be distressed if you have selected quite a few values. We love our values, so pick ten or twelve of your favorites. Of these ten or twelve, write down the four values that are most important (they may be a combination of being and doing values):

MY TOP FOUR CORE VALUES

1. _____

2. _____

3. _____

4. _____

Once you have your top four values in hand, you will be ready to start designing your entire career around them. This is when life gets really fun and exciting, and you'll start to effortlessly attract dynamic people and opportunities.

The Peak Experiences Method

If you are still not certain of your values, think about the best times of your life. Imagine for a moment that you are about to be hit by a bus, and your whole life flashes before your eyes. Imagine taking a gigantic yellow highlighter and coloring in the best times in your life. What would those be? Write down whatever comes to mind, whether that is something that occurred years ago or just recently. Mull over professional or work experiences as well as personal experiences. Think back through your entire life, including your childhood, and jot down the highlights of your life and career. Write as many as you can possibly think of.

Here is a sample list to get you thinking:

HIGHLIGHTS AND PEAK EXPERIENCES

1. Hiking in Malaysia
2. Riding a fast horse on the beach in Mexico
3. Feeling the thrill of giving a presentation
4. Working abroad for one year in Spain

5. Playing in the mud when I was a little kid
6. Taking a road trip around the United States
7. Being named top salesperson of the year
8. Seeing the Grand Canyon
9. Dancing the waltz perfectly to a live band
10. Taking a weeklong yoga retreat
11. Camping in the Arizona mountains
12. Volunteering for the Fresh Air Fund
13. Tutoring El Salvadoran refugees in English
14. Running the New York Marathon
15. Taking an enlightening personal development course
16. Taking a creative drawing class
17. Enjoying an excellent meal out with friends
18. Seeing my first book in print

THE HIGHLIGHTS AND PEAK EXPERIENCES OF MY LIFE

1. _____

2. _____

3. _____

4. _____

5. _____

6. _____

7. _____

8. _____

9. _____

10. _____

11. _____

12. _____

13. _____

14. _____

15. _____

Now go back and review the top values you selected and determine the core value behind each peak experience that you just listed. Don't forget that everyone is unique, so while living abroad in Spain for one year may reflect my value for travel and adventure, for another person it may reflect the lure of the unknown or the value of feeling connected. Two people can have the same experience and value it for very different reasons.

The point is to identify those core values so that you can use that knowledge as a guide in selecting the right career. If the career is aligned with your values, you'll likely find it personally fulfilling and rewarding. If it is in conflict with your values, then you'll likely soon be dissatisfied, frustrated, and unhappy regardless of how much the job pays. Sometimes people can stay in the wrong job for years, but then one day, they just can't stand it anymore, and they quit. The sooner you quit and find the career that matches your values, the happier and more successful you'll be!

SAMPLE HIGHLIGHTS/ PEAK EXPERIENCES	CORE VALUE EXPRESSED
1. Working abroad in Spain	Travel/adventure
2. Giving a presentation	Lead/inspire
3. Decorating home	Beauty
4. Teaching a yoga class	Peace/spiritual
5. Creating a new product	Create/invent

MY HIGHLIGHTS/ PEAK EXPERIENCES	CORE VALUE EXPRESSED
1. _____	_____
2. _____	_____
3. _____	_____

MY HIGHLIGHTS/ PEAK EXPERIENCES	CORE VALUE EXPRESSED
4. _____	_____
5. _____	_____
6. _____	_____
7. _____	_____
8. _____	_____
9. _____	_____
10. _____	_____

Use Your Core Values and Passions to Assess Your Career Options

As advertised, you are now set to start designing your career around your core values and passions. The more closely your career aligns with your core values and passions, the happier and more fulfilled you'll be at work. This is when work truly becomes play. I usually ask my clients to start by creating a values-based project or two, regardless of what else they are doing in their lives. For instance, when I was working at the bank, I decided that in order to express my value to lead and inspire others, I could start by leading the First-Time Home Buyers' Seminar. I wouldn't have wanted to make a career out of this, but it was good practice for speaking in front of an audience.

Let me relate a personal example of the power of core values—this may seem a bit out-there, but it isn't. When I decided I wanted to become a professional speaker (to express my values to lead and inspire), I started by taking courses on how to lead seminars offered by a personal growth and development company. At one point, I had a major disagreement with the trainers' values (they had an aggressive, hard-sell sales strategy that ran counter to my style of attracting clients, which is a natural, soft-sell approach). I decided to lead my own seminars and quit their training program.

I had read once in a Tony Robbins book that he started giving seminars for free out of his tiny apartment. Now he is one of the most highly paid motivational speakers in the world. If Tony could do it, well, then so could I. I started by sending out a one-page invitation printed on brightly colored paper off my home computer for a Sunday-evening potluck supper with a talk, led by me of course, that I called "Life Design." I invited some friends and acquaintances and asked them to bring along a dish of their favorite food as well as their favorite friends. I made a big pot of chili so that there was a main course, and given that this was New York City, most people brought something from a deli—a pizza or Chinese stir-fry—to round out the fare. We started with the food to break the ice, and after that was done, I got up and delivered the presentation for the next hour. Then we broke for dessert and had a final wrap-up. That became my standard format.

I got most of my first paying clients simply by giving this free seminar once a month. I was still working at the bank, so once I got up to sixteen clients, I realized that was too much and went back down to eight until I left Chase. It was a very easy way to get a coaching business off the ground! Then I decided it was time to get out of my tiny apartment, where people had to sit on the bed and on the floor, and get a bit more professional, so I rented a seminar space and began charging for the seminar—I was moving up in the world.

Or was I? To my dismay, only one person attended the first session. I decided to carry on nevertheless and presented the entire seminar to this one woman—who later became a coach herself! I also taped this seminar and used the recording as the basis for the script for my very first product, the *Irresistible Attraction: A Way of Life* audio program, which is still a strong seller after all these years! Now, here is the odd thing . . . somehow word got out that I was leading the *Irresistible Attraction* seminar in New York City, and other organizations asked me if I'd be willing to come and speak at their meetings. To my complete amazement, the National Speakers Association in Kansas City invited me to come and speak for its group of eighty members and paid for my airfare and hotel. I was thrilled! Not only was I speaking, but also I was speaking to professional speakers!

After doing free talks for a while, I started getting invitations from corporations and was flown about to exotic locations to speak at corporate retreats. In addition to those perks, I'd command a decent speaking fee. It felt like getting a paid vacation! This is what I mean about how things start to snowball into a whole new career direction.

Most people don't just wake up one day and find themselves speaking in front of large audiences or doing that dream job. Tony Robbins started out speaking for free to anyone he could get to listen. Now he commands a significant fee for a keynote presentation. Most people start at the very bottom; it is a fine place to start, so don't let that discourage you. It would have been easy for me to say that my first paid seminar was a complete failure, but it wasn't at all. It became the basis for my first product and the start of a successful and lucrative speaking career.

When we lack passion in one area of life, it tends to suck the passion out of every other area. The way to break this vicious circle is to start adding the passion back in. Then the passionless areas are suddenly blatantly obvious, and we naturally start to change those as well. It doesn't matter where you start; just start, however seemingly small or insignificant the change may appear.

How to Orient Your Career Around Your Core Values

The key to ongoing happiness is to orient your career and life around your top core values. Ideally, you want to structure your entire life so that you are living your values all the time, every day. It may take a bit of time to do this (I had to quit my job and start my own business before I could fully express my values to lead and inspire people every day), but the important thing is to start with whatever you can do now. Do not wait any longer. Review your list of peak experiences in life, and see if you can put some of those back into your life on a more regular basis.

Although the step you take here may seem small and insignificant, any step that brings you closer to your values is a step in the right direction. Also, this gesture has a way of compounding quickly once you are on the right path. Even if your particular passion doesn't pay well, it is important that you keep doing the things you love to do. Do not be afraid to take a regular job to pay the bills—such as most actors or artists end up waiting tables to support themselves until they become successful. Sometimes our passions evolve into paying careers. I once saw some striking paintings at a friend's house, and when I expressed my admiration, she told me that the artist used to work at all sorts of odd jobs (taxi driver, plumber, handyman) to make ends meet and support his family. In his spare time he did these unusual paintings. Now he has quite a following and is selling his paintings for thousands of dollars as fast as he can finish them!

And sometimes our passions never become careers. One client, Janette, is an avid ballroom dancer and easily spends $30,000 a year on dance lessons and costumes. At first she was worried about spending so much money on her passion for dance, until she saw that her real estate business grew even faster. Janette gets so much energy from dancing that she attracts much higher-level and more profitable business deals. She has used her passion to give her energy to do her work with greater joy and enthusiasm, and this is vitally important in a sales business. Although Janette has entered and won dance competitions, she does not consider dance her profession—it is her passion.

I want to make it clear that not all people will make money from their passions, but that doesn't mean you shouldn't pursue them. Do whatever you can afford to do now—it is what makes for a fulfilling and exciting life. Think about the things you can do right now, starting today, that express your core values and passions.

Here is an example from my life:

ACTIONS	VALUE EXPRESSED
1. Keynote conference in India	Travel/adventure/lead and inspire
2. Horseback riding	Fun/play
3. Write a book	Create/inspire
4. Meditate	Balance/spirituality
5. Volunteer at a charity	Contribute

When you move into alignment with your core values, wonderful things start to happen. When you are doing what you love to do, you'll be enjoying yourself and feeling fully alive, and people will notice the change. You will have more energy and be more joyful, leading you to a more productive process as you assess your desired career change or job transition.

Are Your Values Compatible with Your Prospective Employer's Values?

Once you've identified your own values, it makes sense to see whether they are compatible with those of your prospective employers—and I don't mean the phony values that they outline in the company report. What do they really value? Does the company have a genuine reputation for supporting working parents? Is it really an environmentally green company, or do people there just go through the motions and not even recycle the paper? If you want to have a family, and the company doesn't have any existing examples of having supported other working parents by setting them up to telecommute or job share or by providing excellent day care, then you may end up quitting.

Use the formats provided here to enter your responses:

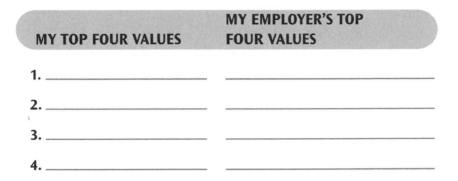

MY TOP FOUR VALUES	MY EMPLOYER'S TOP FOUR VALUES
1. _____	_____
2. _____	_____
3. _____	_____
4. _____	_____

PROJECTS/ACTIVITIES THAT EXPRESS MY TOP CORE VALUES

1. _____

2. _____

3. _____

4. _____

Start That Values-Based Goal or Project Now!

Your values shape your future, and many of us defer living our values and, therefore, our future. In truth, one of the best ways to attract the perfect career is to start doing all the things you've imagined you'd do when you had more time or more money. (Look back to the "If Money Were No Object" exercise in Step 3.) It helps to start with a few items from your list of things you'd do if money were no object. My client Melissa Todd said that on her list of things she'd do if she had a million dollars was "Live in Napa and taste wines." She didn't have a million, but then it also didn't cost a million to rent a place for a month and go to one winery after another! Another client always wanted to own a sailboat, and I suggested that he simply rent one and go sailing for a day as a starting point—easily done and within his budget, whereas owning a sailboat was not.

Don't wait until you have the time and money, because by then you may be too old to enjoy it. If you are interviewing and facing rejection, doing something you like will give you pleasure and energy, making you more attractive to your potential employer.

What about travel? Have you been thinking about the places you'd like to go once you have a stable job? You don't have to wait until your ship comes in to start traveling. You can fly as a courier for a nominal fee. Volunteer for a charity abroad. There are loads of ways to work and travel: join the Marines, take up travel writing, teach English abroad, work on a cruise ship. One client said she wanted to go to Italy but was waiting for someone to travel with. I said she should go anyway, and she did and ended up meeting her future husband there! Stop waiting to live, and get out there now!

Are you waiting until you stumble across the perfect career or job? Don't quit your day job while you start your search for the ideal career. Use your evenings and weekends to launch your home-based business or to take courses that interest you. Simplify your life and downsize if necessary so that you'll be able to afford to take some risks and experiment with going back to school for new training or start writing that novel. Don't wait until the moment is just right. Now is the time to enroll in those evening classes or to start moonlighting with a sideline business.

Take a Course or Class That Energizes You and Plays to Your Ideal Career

Try taking a class that leaves you energized and full of vitality. Have a go at ballroom, swing, or salsa dancing. Take a creative writing class. Sign up for tennis lessons. Give pottery, painting, or woodworking a whirl—whatever appeals to you. People can tell just by looking at you whether you are lit up and enjoying life or are pallid and gray from sitting at home in front of the TV or surfing the Net. You too can stand out from a crowd. Just start doing something that makes you feel absolutely fabulous.

In the space provided in this section, draw up your own list of activities that light you up, turn you on, and make you feel alive and wonderful. This is essential information if you are interviewing for a job and can make the difference between being hired or not. If you are starting your own business, you'll need

> *An effort impelled by desire must also have an automatic or subconscious energy to aid its realization.*
>
> —MAN RAY

to be energized and attractive to prospective clients—so, if you are feeling down in the dumps or just plain exhausted, it is time to find something fun that gives you energy and makes you feel alive. Doing so is more important than you realize. This dynamic isn't a mystery. Imagine you are interviewing two candidates, both currently unemployed, for the same job opening, and they are in all respects equally qualified. One candidate has stopped all the fun and exciting activities in her life, because she didn't think she could afford them anymore, while the other candidate has kept up her passion for dancing. Which one will get the job? My money is on the dancer, because she'll show up more energized, radiant, and full of joy and vigor.

Write down as many ideas as you can think of, and then pick one or two to get started with right away. Again, do this now. (I hope you are getting the message.)

1. _____

2. _____

3. _____

4. _____

5. _____

6. _____

7. _____

8. _____

9. _____

10. _____

Classrooms are also a promising setting to meet a variety of people, including potential contacts for a new career or clients for your start-up business. Moonlight and experiment with a new business idea in the evenings and weekends. Take a creative writing class and get working on that book or screenplay. If you think you don't have time now, just unplug the TV and hide it in the back of a closet. That usually frees up an instant twenty hours a week—enough time to take evening classes and retrain for a new career, get a hobby or small business going, or moonlight in an activity that interests you.

Make another list right now of all the things you've been waiting to do when the economy improves, or when you get a good income, or when you have more time. I've worked with a number of clients who, when they finally did have more time (because they were downsized), wasted that precious time instead of actually doing the things they said they'd do if they had time, such as travel to a foreign country or volunteer for an organization they admire. I realize you may well not have money right now, but you do have time, so take advantage of this fact to do those things that take time—the crafting class, putting the photo albums together, learning a new skill or language. You can do this and still work part-time if you must to generate some income while you are searching for the perfect work or career.

WHEN I HAVE MORE TIME OR MONEY I'LL . . .

1. _____

2. _____

3. _____

4. _____

5. _____

6. _____

Good! Now pick one of the activities you've been putting off that is an expression of one of your top four values, and start doing it. You may need to choose the low-cost, affordable option to start, but don't let that deter you from getting up off the couch.

Identifying and living your values and passions will help you understand and identify your perfect career or job. Also, being excited by the activity will make you feel turned on and excited about your life. The more excited you are about life, the more attractive you will be to prospective employers, managers, and/or clients. So, start now. If you love your life now, you'll be much more engaging to your future employer, and you may find that you can turn your passion into a viable business. Start that special values-based project that inspires you—now!

SUCCESS STORY

The Banking Executive Who Broke Through the Glass Ceiling

One of my clients, let's call her Catherine to protect her identity given the sensitive nature of this story, hired me when she was working at a major U.S. bank as a senior vice president of marketing and sales. She was frustrated with her job because of the corporate politics and the old boys' network, which she couldn't seem to crack. Her boss complimented her work, but she had to fight for everything she wanted to do. On the plus side, the job paid well, and she had a top-notch team of people working for her. She received an offer from her prior company, another major U.S. bank; her old boss wanted her back and offered her a position there as head of sales and marketing and a slightly higher salary package. She hemmed and hawed and wasn't sure what to do. Then, on one of our calls she told me about the unbelievable behavior of a senior executive with whom she worked. He struck one of her employees with a cane. Thank heavens there was a witness in the room: a secretary had seen it happen. Catherine didn't know what to do. Her employee was mortified (and probably scared to death) and didn't want her to say anything at all about the event.

I pointed out to Catherine that as his boss, she had an obligation to protect him from physical abuse in the workplace and that knowing what she knew, she had to report this outrageous behavior. She couldn't cover it up without becoming liable herself. Taking action required tremendous courage on her part, and she was certain this incident would derail her career and possibly get her fired herself. In short, ratting on the big boss was not something that she was keen on doing. She took the courageous step of reporting this event to human resources in spite of her employee's concerns. An internal investigation ensued, during which other employees came forth and spoke of similar abuses, and thankfully, the offender was terminated.

Given the clearly appalling work conditions, it would seem obvious that she should jump at the new job offer with open arms, but Catherine still couldn't decide whether to accept the position at her former bank. My advice was that she shouldn't take the new offer until she was jumping up and down for joy. I said, "If they want you and are coming to you with an offer, then you are in a great position to ask for what you really want." Then I suggested, "Make a list of everything you want that would get you really excited about taking the job, and make a huge request." Catherine knew that in order to really do what she wanted to do, she'd need a bigger title. With the title comes respect, power, and influence (not to mention better perks). She made a list of about ten conditions she would need to have met in order to accept the offer, including bringing her assistant with her and getting the executive vice president title, among a host of other terms. She got almost everything she asked for on her list of ten! At that point, she was jumping for joy and took the job.

Talane interviews her client, Catherine:

What was the biggest shift for you?

It was making a huge and outrageous request and getting it. I realized that I wouldn't be happy taking a job that wasn't big enough and challenging enough. I didn't want to make another lateral move at this point in my career, even if that meant getting out of a really negative situation.

What was your biggest challenge?

I've had to keep on making big requests at the bank to get what I needed in order to do the job properly. When my requests were approved, then I knew they were really behind me and that I had the support to get the work done. We are now one of the few banks in the United States that haven't been bought out by the government.

What was the best outcome from your career transition?

I have created a coaching culture at the bank. Even the finance department talks about coaching now. All of the managers and their teams have gone through the computerized assessments, and they manage around developing people's strengths, not focusing on their weaknesses. I'm pleased to have made that kind of impact in the company.

How did you overcome your fear of change?

In the end, you have to live with yourself. I knew I had to do the right thing and report the abusive behavior of this senior executive even though it could have destroyed my own career. I'm pleased to say that it actually had the reverse effect, and my career has skyrocketed to the top. It took every bit of courage that I had, but it was the right thing to do.

As for the fear of taking the new job, my fears were right on target and were stopping me for a very good reason. If I had accepted the job at the lower title, I would not have had the respect and power I needed to really make the impact I wanted. I needed the chairman

*and board to respect me from the beginning, and that meant start-
ing at the right level, not working my way up to that point. Once the
job offer was right, the fear disappeared, and it was easy to make
the jump, because I was jumping for joy! Thanks to your coaching,
I held out and got the offer I really wanted. You didn't let me settle
for less. If I had settled, I can see now I would have been miserable.*

**What personal advice would you like to give others who also want
to transition in their careers?**

*Make huge and what will feel to you like outrageous requests, and be
prepared to cite your reasons for those requests. I knew exactly why
I needed that title, and when I asked for it, there wasn't one single
quaver in my voice. I was confident and firm. People can sense when
you mean business and are not going to back down on something.
When I got it clearly in my head that this was what I needed to
accept the offer, it was nonnegotiable for me.*

Putting It All Together

Create Your Career Profile and Life Plan

The reason most people never reach their goals is that they don't define them, or ever seriously consider them as believable or achievable. Winners can tell you where they are going, what they plan to do along the way, and who will be sharing the adventure with them.

—DENNIS WAITLEY

At this point, you've identified your personal requirements, you're clear on your passions and values, you know what your natural talents and abilities are, and you know your personal style. This next step is to think about where you are in your life and create a rough outline or sketch of your life plan so you can create a career profile that makes sense given where you are right now. The stage of your life is the final piece of the puzzle and may affect which career is the best choice for you

> *When love and skill work together, expect a masterpiece.*
>
> —JOHN RUSKIN

now. In this chapter, you will create your own unique career profile by pulling all these pieces together to produce the big picture. This will form the guiding vision for your various careers or business ventures throughout your life. This is your "core"—the essentially hardwired parts of you that are likely to remain the same for the rest of your life. What will change: the different sorts of careers that are available, the businesses you might choose to start, and your passions and values as we grow and change. After all, who knew twenty years ago that we'd need Web designers?

What's Important to Me Now?

Before you create your career profile, I invite you to think about your current life and objectives. There are lots of careers to choose from and possible businesses to start, but where you are in life right now may be the deciding factor as to why you choose one line of work over another. This is the question to which the answer will vary over a lifetime, because what is important to you now may be very different from what is important to you as years go by. When you are just graduating from college, you may be willing and even be excited to take an eighty-hour-a-week job and may thrive on it, but I've yet to meet anyone getting ready to retire who wants to work that many hours. This is the time to think of your life plan. A life plan helps you plot a course over your entire life. For example, if you want to do something athletic, it makes sense to do it early in life when you are young and strong, as you probably won't make the Olympic team when you are ninety. Likewise, it is much easier to have children before you are forty—not that it can't be done

> *Men, for the sake of getting a living, forget to live.*
>
> —MARGARET FULLER

later (as I'm proof of the pudding); it is just that it is easier and less risky for both mother and child. Also, I've coached many executive women who got so busy in their careers that they lost track of time, and when they finally came up for air, it was too late to have children.

Making a life plan, even if it is a coarse outline or a few bullet points scratched down, and referring back to it every year or so is a good way to ensure that you don't miss the chance to do the things in life that are really important to you. The life-planning exercise is fun and relatively easy for those who can imagine the future, but if your brain thinks only six months to a year ahead, this could be a difficult if not impossible task. Not everyone has the ability to imagine the future—your brain may not go there. So, just do the best you can to sketch out a few rough ideas of what you'd like to accomplish in life. I've given two options for creating a life plan and you can do whichever you prefer or do both for good measure. If you are really stuck, work with a coach who can help you create a bigger life plan.

Create Your Life Plan

As a culture, we are so career focused that we tend to forget that the purpose of working is to support our ideal life. The pursuit of money has become an end in itself. While I like to have money just as much as the next person (if not more!), there is no amount of money that is worth sacrificing your life for. As our lives change, our require-ments and values can change as well. It isn't always easy to predict just how things will turn out. I've coached super ambitious executive women who were certain that they'd be right back to work after having children and then, much to their own surprise, had a complete change of values and decided to become stay-at-home mothers and loved it. I personally thought I'd be a full-time, stay-at-home mother, but after breast-feeding for nine months, I was eager to get back into coaching—I was hungry for mental challenges and stimulation.

> *You have to be very careful if you don't know where you are going because you might not get there.*
>
> —YOGI BERRA

I particularly like the example (in Step 4) of my client who was a professional musician and had his own band, but got tired of being on the road after doing it for twenty-plus years and decided to become a nurse instead. He enrolled in nursing school in his forties. Even the die-hard rock stars can get tired of doing the same thing all the time. Every now and then it makes sense to sit back and exam-ine the big picture of your life—take stock of where you've been and where you'd like to go. If you don't make a few plans, it is easy to drift through life or get really busy, and before you know it, you'll have missed the oppor-

> *The hardest years in life are those between ten and seventy.*
>
> —HELEN HAYES AT AGE EIGHTY-THREE

tunity to do what you really wanted to do and your life will be over and there is no getting it back. Once again, take a few min-utes here to jot down and compile your answers from the prior chapters so you can see how it all starts to come together, and then consider where you are right now in the grand scheme of things.

"Life Without Regrets" List

This exercise is particularly helpful for people who feel they have to do everything right away and overload their schedules trying to get it all done this year. This pattern only leads to their being stressed and overwhelmed and not enjoying the things they want to do simply because they are doing too much. By spreading your major goals and objectives out over a lifetime, you can relax and enjoy each stage of your life. I have to remind myself of this as well. I have two little girls under the age of five, and these are the intense child-raising years. Soon they will be in school, and this time will pass, never to be recouped. I have a five-year window in which to really appreciate and enjoy them. As a result, I've dropped my French lessons and plans to travel for the time being, and instead we are focusing on more family-oriented activities that we can all enjoy, such as camping.

Time is the thing that keeps everything from happening all at once at the same time.

—ANONYMOUS

List the things you want to make sure you do before you die. (For example: see the Great Wall of China, learn to write poetry, have children, find my soul mate, leave a legacy, grow an herb garden, become masterful in my career, learn how to tango.) Jot down whatever comes to mind here in no particular order or priority.

1. _____

2. _____

3. _____

4. _____

5. _____

6. _____

7. _____

8. _____

9. _____

10. _____

11. _____

12. _____

13. _____

14. _____

15. _____

For every stage of your life, there are things that you'll find more enjoyable. Studying French was impossible when I was exhausted and brain-dead from breast-feeding through the night. In a few years, it may be fun again, but for now, it isn't even on the list. I've got that roughly penciled in for when I'm about sixty-five and I take a year off to live in Paris, paint, study French, and laze around playing the Bohemian.

The point of this exercise is to see that yes, you *can* have it all, just not all at once! Now take the things you definitely want to do in your life from the preceding list and jot them down in the decade that seems most appropriate for your life. Don't worry about getting this perfect as things will most certainly change. Things you think are interesting when you are twenty may have no appeal at all when you are sixty. And things are changing so quickly that there may be activities or options you can't conceive of now that will be available in the future. So just sketch in a rough outline of the things you really want to make sure you do in this life and when you'd like to do them. (I've filled in the background to get you started, but feel free to change it.) Alternatively, you can skip this step if it seems too hard and simply make a visual map of your life plan instead.

DECADES OF MY LIFE	POSSIBLE ACTIVITIES/GOALS
0–9 years	Play/learn
10–19 years	School/learn
20s	School/work
30s	_____
40s	_____
50s	_____
60s	_____
70s	_____
80s	_____
90s	_____
100+ years	_____

Annual Life Plan

Now that you have the big picture, you can work on creating a plan for this year. Here is a sample of what your annual life plan might contain (feel free to add any other elements that you'd like to incorporate). Jot down your answers below or write each on a separate index card. (You can also download a free Life Planner from Lifecoach.com.)

BIG GOALS

A big goal is something that would typically take six months to a year to achieve, so ideally choose only one or two big goals a year. For example, my big goal this year was to write this book, and I have smaller projects running as well.

1. _____

2. _____

PROJECTS

These are usually smaller tasks or objectives that won't take a year to complete such as writing the first chapter of a book, building a deck, learning how to make great minestrone, making a movie of your kids, etc. At least one of your projects will be supporting your big goal.

1. _____

2. _____

3. _____

PEOPLE TO BEFRIEND, SPEND MORE TIME WITH, OR GET CLOSER TO

People could include family members, coworkers, friends, etc.

1. _____

2. _____

3. _____

NEW SKILLS TO LEARN

These could include learning tennis, cyberskills, art, etc.

1. _____

2. _____

3. _____

PROBLEMS TO RESOLVE

Issues could include getting out of debt, asking for an apology, negotiating a peace, etc.

1. _____

2. _____

3. _____

FABULOUS ADVENTURES OR VACATIONS

These could include trips, holidays, new places to see or explore, fun things to do, etc.

1. _____

2. _____

3. _____

4. _____

5. _____

THINGS TO LET GO OF OR COMPLETE

Forgive those who have harmed you, pay off any personal debts, apologize for any harm done—whether intentional or not—get off that committee, resign from volunteer jobs you no longer enjoy, etc.

1. _____

2. _____

3. _____

Under each big goal (or on the flip side of the index card), jot down five to ten possible ways you could achieve each goal. You may wish to declare a theme for the year that would guide your choices and actions. You might choose to set a theme for "fun and adventure" if things have gotten a bit dull lately, or "romance" to strengthen your love and relationships, or "health and vitality" if you are feeling run down. Align your theme to one of your top core values and you can't go wrong. Select whichever theme most inspires you. Then when you make decisions about whether or not to do something over the course of the year, you can ask yourself if it is aligned with your chosen theme. (After giving birth to my second daughter and breast-feeding for months, my husband and I decided we needed to declare a year for fun!)

Create a Visual Map of Your Life Plan

If you are struggling with the previous exercise, or it seems entirely impossible and you just can't imagine in which decade you'll be doing what, then try this instead. In fact, even if you have done the above exercise, do this one as well if it appeals to you. Having a visual reminder of your goals is a very powerful tool. Get a bulletin board, some corkboard, or a whiteboard; push pins or tacks; and a bunch of old magazines, index cards, and envelopes to make a visual map of your life plan. Pin up all the images of things you'd like to do in your lifetime. For example, you might clip out that photo of the Great Wall of China from an old *National Geographic* magazine if that represents your desire to walk the wall some day, a photo of a baby or two if you want children, a photo of that house or that holiday destination you dream of. Post any images that represent the things you want to make sure you achieve in this lifetime. Don't worry about the decade and instead just make this your plan. You can then easily add, change, or swap the images as your interests or desires change. In the middle of the board, write down your goals for this year—use an image as well that represents your goal or theme for the year.

If some of your goals require money, tack up an envelope with the name of that goal written on the outside. As unexpected or additional sums of cash come your way, pop the bills into that envelope. You can even paste the picture of what you want to the outside of the envelope. For example, let's say you want to go on a holiday to Greece but don't have any money saved. Put up a photo of Greece and an envelope that says "Vacation in Greece," and pin that up to your bulletin board as well. You'll be amazed at how quickly you'll reach your objectives simply by using this simple visual reminder. Make sure you hang the bulletin board where you can see it every day.

I do this exercise at the start of each new year, but there is no time like the present, so don't wait. When I do this in late December or early January each year, I first make a list of all my accomplishments, large and small, over the past year and read each accomplishment out loud. I take out my day planner to review the year as it is so easy to forget everything that I've done. (By the way, this is a great exercise to share with your family or friends, but also can be done alone.) Most people are too quick to think of their new goals and neglect to appreciate and savor all the wonderful things they have already accomplished. Take stock of what you've already done and pat yourself on the back (or better yet, get your friends and family to acknowledge you!) before you start thinking of what you want to do next. You can always use the start of each new year and/or your birthday to reevaluate your objectives and make changes. Have fun with this exercise! You might even make a postholiday or New Year's party of it and invite friends over to do the same. Ask them to bring a pair of scissors and a bunch of old magazines they don't mind cutting up.

Now let's work on your career profile so that we can see how that fits into your new life plan.

Get Out of the Box: List Five Alternative Careers

Sometimes we need to break through our limited beliefs about what we think we can do or have. I was recently giving a seminar for my alumni club in London, and one of the fellows there was an unemployed hedge fund manager. He loved his job. He couldn't imagine doing anything else. Well, the current state of the economy meant that hedge funds were an endangered species and that no matter how hard he looked, he probably wasn't going to find work in his old field. It's not unusual for people to get so caught up in one field or career that they can't conceive of an equally fitting alternative. The truth is that our skills and talents are transferable to many different careers.

> *There is no security on this earth; there is only opportunity.*
>
> —GENERAL DOUGLAS MACARTHUR

Imagine that your job has been eliminated from the face of the planet. There are no more hedge funds to manage. In the space provided, write down at least five alternative careers. What else could you do? Look back to your list of talents, skills, and values, and write down all the possible careers you can think of that sound like fun. Don't sweat it; you don't have to suit up to do any or all of these. The point is to get you thinking about possible options.

MY CAREER PROFILE

Think of the career profile as your template to help you determine whether a specific job will be ultimately satisfying to you and worth pursuing. Without this template, you may end up accepting a job that looks good but ultimately takes you off the best track and leaves you feeling frustrated, stuck, unfulfilled, or miserable. The career profile is your touchstone to help you make the best career decisions in life. By knowing all the elements of yourself, you'll be able to select a career or start a business with confidence, assured that you are hardwired to be brilliant at that particular activity. This knowledge will give you both power and confidence—good things to have when going on an interview or opening your own business! This will help you see how you *can* have it all— just maybe not all at the same time. Collect and review all of the pertinent information you've gathered about yourself, resulting from the exercises you've done in the previous chapters and put them together to create a career profile here. If you've skipped some of the steps, it will be obvious which ones you need to go back and review.

My Personal Requirements
List your top four needs. (Exercise from Step 2)

1. _____

2. _____

3. _____

4. _____

My Ideal Working Environment
Describe your ideal work environment. Include the working conditions, hours, environment, types of people you work

continued

with or for, amount of money you'd like to make, the kind of boss or manager you'd like to work for, and so on. The more specific, the better! (Exercise from Step 3)

_____

_____

_____

_____

_____

_____

My Unique Talents and Natural Abilities
List your natural strengths, talents, and abilities. (Exercise from Step 4)

1. _____

2. _____

3. _____

4. _____

5. _____

My Envy List
List what you secretly want for yourself but think you can't have. (Exercise from Step 5)

1. _____

2. _____

3. _____

4. _____

5. _____

My Values and Passions List

List your top five to ten values and passions. (Exercise from Step 5)

1. _____

2. _____

3. _____

4. _____

5. _____

6. _____

7. _____

8. _____

9. _____

10. _____

My Favorite Skills and Hobbies

List all your favorite skills—things you've learned to do that you enjoy doing, such as typing, cooking gourmet meals, negotiating deals, selling, managing, reading, investigating, decorating the house, spotting antiques, or playing the piano. This may be a long list! Go ahead and write down everything

continued

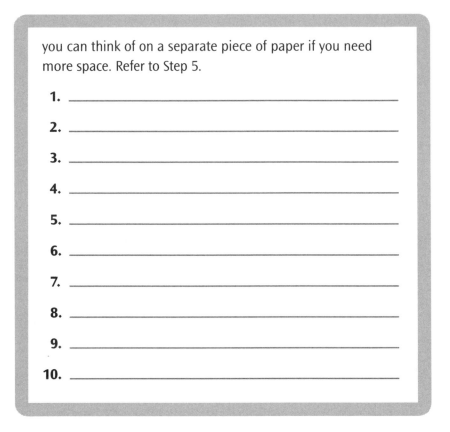

you can think of on a separate piece of paper if you need
more space. Refer to Step 5.

1. _____

2. _____

3. _____

4. _____

5. _____

6. _____

7. _____

8. _____

9. _____

10. _____

This insight comes in handy if you have both the talent and desire
for a number of different careers. For instance, you may equally
enjoy landscape gardening and interior design, but currently there
is a need in your community for garden design, so that is what you
do now.

My previously mentioned rock-star client who wanted to do
something different had first thought of becoming a music therapist, which would have suited his talents, skills, and abilities
perfectly. However, he couldn't get work as a music therapist while
being a drummer, and it is a very hard field to break into. So, he
took the practical option of becoming a nurse, which would allow
him to start as soon as he finished his nursing training and for
which jobs are plentiful and pay well.

MY ALTERNATIVE CAREERS

1. _____

2. _____

3. _____

4. _____

5. _____

It's OK to Take a Minibreak or Sabbatical

If you just can't seem to figure things out or are stumped by these exercises, it may be time to take a break from your routine and get some perspective on your life. It may be that you pack it all in to volunteer for the Peace Corps for a year or two, or it may simply be that you book a three-day weekend at a B and B in the vicinity. Sometimes we are so immersed in our current lives, family commitments, and work that we just can't train our eyes on the bigger picture. I strongly recommend that at a minimum you book that long weekend away. That is often enough of a restorative,

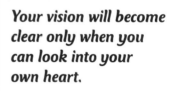

Your vision will become clear only when you can look into your own heart.

—CARL JUNG

but if it isn't, then you can consider doing something a tad more extreme such as taking an extended leave of absence or a proper sabbatical.

During these tough times, you may think it's impossible to take a long-term sabbatical, and that's OK, but there are numerous other ways to take a retreat from your life. Besides staying at a B and B for a weekend, you could spend a few days at an inn in a small town, a quiet beach house during the off-season, or a cabin in the woods. You might house-sit for a friend who is traveling. The unifying theme here is to make a concerted effort to get out of your own house. You are easy to find there, for one thing, and you just have too many distractions—something always needs doing in our own digs. When you are in someone else's house, the fact that the eaves need painting isn't going to bother you, because it isn't your problem.

Try to go away for at least three days if you can, but if you can't, even one day off the beaten path can make a difference. Many monasteries allow people to stay for free or for a small donation. Pack light: a simple bag with minimal clothes, a journal to record your thoughts, and that is about it. The point is to get away from it all—not drag it all along with you. Turn your cell phone off, and don't watch TV or surf the Internet. This is your time to be with your own thoughts, so give yourself a reprieve from the newspapers and magazines and the news broadcasts. When I lived in New York City, I used to take weekends to go to the Shivananda Yoga Ranch. It was inexpensive and rustic. One time they had a silent weekend, and we weren't allowed to speak for the duration. That was a wonderful and calming experience for someone who likes to talk!

All the same, it may be that you flat-out don't have the time, energy, or money to leave your home even for a weekend. Let's say you don't have the vacation time left, or the mere thought of going anywhere exhausts you: then take a miniretreat in your own abode. Tell your friends and family that you are going to be away, and then unplug your phone, hide your TV, and make your home into a minispa. Start each day with a special ritual, and when you come home from work, light a candle, meditate, or take a hot bath and let the stresses of the day drain away. Try to eliminate the petty annoyances. Get your bill-paying out of the way, just as you would do before leaving on a real vacation, so that you can free your mind to think and relax. Spend some time in nature if you can. Go for long walks, listen to music, write in your journal, get a massage.

If there are family members in your home, you'll have to take a retreat without them. If necessary, ask someone to take the kids for a weekend so that you have more than two minutes to get your thoughts together. Leave your partner behind too—you need to sort this out yourself, and a little absence will do your relationship good and make you appreciate each other more. We all need time alone now and then, even the extroverts. Do what you must, but make sure you get some perspective on your life, so that you can think about your job and the kind of career you'd like to pursue.

Design the Ideal Career or Business

Now that you've created your unique career profile, you may want to rework or expand on the Ideal Job Description you jotted down in Step 3 so that it more accurately reflects your profile. Are there any changes you'd now make, given your deeper understanding of what you are wired to do? Rework and embellish your ideal career description on the following pages until you think, "Wow! This would be a dream come true!" You can always change it later on as your personal requirements, passions, and values evolve over time. Ideally, review your needs and values every decade of your life to ensure that your goals are in alignment with your passions and values.

> *I used to work at the International House of Pancakes. It was a dream, and I made it happen.*
>
> —PAULA POUNDSTONE

If you do nothing else, *do* this exercise! It is immeasurably powerful. Just to give you an example, when I was working at the bank, making $30,000 a year and feeling that there had to be something better for me, I drafted (on my coach's orders) an ideal job description. At the time I wrote it, I thought it represented the most pie-in-the-sky impossible thing to have in the world. After you read it, you'll see that I hadn't even imagined I could own my own business and work for myself as a coach. Nor did I think big enough incomewise. Now I have all this and even more! So, think big— really big! And remember, this is your *ideal* job description.

It may take time before you get all the various components together, so don't panic if this exact job doesn't appear instantly, but rather use this as your vision for the future; accept jobs and take actions that move you ever closer to this ideal. I've kept my original description, which I jotted down in my Filofax, and will share it here as an illustration. My version is mostly in bullet form. Some clients have written out whole pages in vivid detail. Others cut out pictures from magazines to make a collage of their dream career. However you prefer to do it, invest a few minutes to draft out your own ideal job description. Remember to make sure it supports your ideal life and is aligned with your values and passions. Use the work you've done in this chapter and from prior chapters to help you custom-tailor it exactly to your unique talents, desires, and your ideal life.

TALANE'S IDEAL JOB DESCRIPTION

I wrote the following when I was twenty-eight, working as a sales manager for Chase in New York and feeling very frustrated. At the time I wrote this, I had no idea I would become a coach or that coaching was a viable profession, as hardly anyone had even heard of life coaching!

An International Career and Lifestyle: To have an international career requiring extended stays in warm foreign countries such as Brazil, Argentina, Greece, etc. Sales, lucrative, exciting.
    Here are the components that I associated with my ideal career:

International consultant
Presentations (energy flow, sharing)
Coaching
High-level creative (not technical)
Working with business executives, middle- and senior-level
    management
Living in foreign countries

Travel around the world with extended stays of one month
to a year in warm countries
Opportunity to learn new languages—French, Portuguese,
Italian
Salary $100,000 base with bonus for excellence
Negotiation
Selling an excellent product or service

Description of my perfect job: I would love my work to
enable me to continually grow and develop myself—where
there are no limits to how quickly I can advance. My work
is a contribution to others and makes for a happier world.
Independence and freedom to be creative. Support from
my company so I can do my job—tools, developing skills,
training, coaching. Love the people I work with. Respect and
admire my boss.

You've seen how my clients and I have successfully used these
exercises to change careers—now it's your turn to design your
ideal career or business. Write your own perfect job description;
write it down in as much detail as possible in the space provided
here. The more specific, the better!

MY IDEAL CAREER/BUSINESS DESCRIPTION

Now list the steps that would take you one step closer to this ideal. Such as, in my case: hire a coach, sign up for Coach U's coach training program, sign up for Toastmaster's, start leading seminars once a month, get business cards printed, buy a computer.

ACTION PLAN

1. _____

2. _____

3. _____

4. _____

5. _____

6. _____

7. _____

8. _____

9. _____

10. _____

Congratulations! You've done it! Now that you've taken the time to clarify and define who you are and what you want, it is time to start making that ideal come true! Read on for the next step in making the transition to your new career or starting that business you've always dreamed of.

Managing the Transition Smoothly

If you have built castles in the air,
your work need not be lost; that is
where they should be. Now put the
foundations under them.

—HENRY DAVID THOREAU

I f you have not already landed the perfect job in the course of doing the preceding exercises, then you may be wondering how to manage the transition period. Of course, if you have received a handsome severance package or are independently wealthy, you won't need to worry about holding down a day job while you transition to your dream job or get your own business up and running. The rest of us need this chapter. While some people can afford to just start a business or resign a job and leisurely look about for the perfect career, others have families to support or rent to pay and don't have the liberty to stop doing what they are currently doing. If you fall into this category, do not despair! You have plenty of company.

When I started coaching, I was still working full-time at Chase, paying outrageous Manhattan rent, paying off credit card debts, and also saving money to start my business. My case is the norm rather than the exception. Most of us simply don't have the luxury of not working for an extended period. In this chapter, I will share some tips on how to shine at your current job while taking steps toward creating your ideal career. Mindful that you probably won't have oodles of idle hours during this transition period, I'll start by helping you cut out the time wasters so you'll have the freedom to make the transition to the work you love.

Free Up Your Time

One prerequisite to managing your career transition is freeing up your time. You need to make the time to figure out your ideal career and plan your corresponding actions. Cut out all superfluous activities by automating and streamlining your life. You'll be working one and a half or even two jobs. It's not as dire as it may sound: you will

How beautiful it is to do nothing, and then rest afterward.

—SPANISH PROVERB

still have plenty of time to play with friends and family, but you definitely won't have any time to waste. If you are starting your own business, you'll be glad you set up the structures to automate your life now so you can focus on your plans—a new business can be as demanding as a new baby when you are just starting out. See my first book as well, *Coach Yourself to Success*, for ideas on creating more time.

Leverage the 80/20 Rule to Create Even More Time

The object here is to get your current job done in two hours a day so you can use the rest of your time to think about your new career or business. If you are too busy, you won't have time to start building your own business or even to find a better job somewhere else. Don't worry that your performance will suffer; every client I've ever coached to get the job done faster has only been seen as more valuable by the employer. This is the power of using the 80/20 rule—the principle that we get 80 percent of our results from 20 percent of our time investment. If you can identify the 20 percent that matters, you can safely eliminate about 80 percent of what you are currently doing.

I wasn't willing to experiment with this principle until I was willing to be fired. Much to my disbelief, when I did this at my old job, they didn't want me to leave. I practically had to beg them to let me take the severance package! You will still be doing 100 percent grade-A work for your current employer and not slacking off. You'll just be doing what is really important and makes a difference and be letting the unimportant stuff go. You may be surprised to discover how much you don't have to do that you thought you had to. You'll also be working much more efficiently in order to get your work done sooner.

One client was determined to get caught up on her work, so she went in every Saturday for a full month. She realized that she had more work than she could finish in one week, so she'd either have to continue to work six days out of every seven or get rid of some of her tasks. She asked her boss about a particularly time-consuming report and was astounded to be told she didn't have to do it.

It also is important that you manage how you are perceived by your boss and colleagues. In other words, don't be blabbing it around the office that you are working only two hours a day so that you can concentrate on your exciting new business or personal project. Better to keep things under wraps and make sure you do an excellent job (see Step 1). Matthew, a thirty-four-year-old computer programmer, was using slow times between projects at his current job to work on writing a book. He had been making steady progress until he spilled the beans and told some coworkers he was doing NANORIMO (nanorimo.org)—a project that requires writing fifty thousand words in one month in your spare time. Everyone in the office was supportive of his writing project and kept asking him every day how many words he was up. Because there was so much attention on him, he didn't dare write a single sentence while at work, for fear that his colleagues and manager would think he wasn't toeing the line. So, he actually made better progress when no one knew what he was doing. Whatever you do, you need to make it look as if you are working just as hard as, if not harder than, everyone else. You may think it sounds impossible, but if you determinedly focus on the 20 percent, you'll be more productive for the company, not less.

One client, who worked eighty hours a week in mergers and acquisitions at a major U.S. bank, had recently married and was frustrated that he never had time to eat dinner with his new wife. To remedy the situation, he went so far as to move to an apartment that was a ten-minute walk from his office in Manhattan, eliminating a thirty- to forty-minute commute to New Jersey. Then, when he went for dinner, he didn't tell his colleagues he was going home to dine with his wife; instead, he left his coat on the back of his chair, his light turned on at his desk, and his work in progress and mumbled something about talking with so-and-so in such and such department. He'd proceed to go home and have an enjoyable dinner with his wife and then come back and put in another hour or two until everyone left at about eleven P.M. As an unexpected side bonus, he was actually more productive after this much-needed mental break. Now, that is a notable example of managing appearances and working smarter! Remember, if you can't carve out some time for yourself, you'll be blocked from finding a new career or starting a new business.

Eliminate All the Big Time Wasters

> *You will never "find" time for anything. If you want time you must make it.*
>
> —CHARLES BUXTON

Unplug the TV. On average, people watch twenty-four hours of TV a week. If you hide the TV in the closet, you'll be dumbstruck at how much extra time you suddenly have to focus on finding your new career or starting that business. Encourage the whole family to detach from the TV and engage in other activities as a way to support you in your new venture. If family members won't participate, then move the TV to a room where you won't be tempted.

Automate, Systematize, and Delegate

It takes some time to set up the systems needed to handle the time-consuming tasks of modern life, but once you've done it, you'll reap the benefits for years to come. You need to free up as much time as possible from mundane daily tasks in order to create the time for the job search, for getting new training, or for starting your own business. It is well worth the initial investment up front for the long-run savings in time. If you haven't set up bill-paying online or automatic debits, do it now! This is one task that is time-consuming and easy to automate.

Another way to create more time for yourself is to teach the kids how to do the laundry and cook simple meals. It will help them in the long run, as they'll need to learn this stuff eventually.

If you have very young children, get more creative about lining up babysitters, including getting friends, family, and even neighbors to help out. One of my friends sets up playdates for her daughter that last four hours. She either pays the other parent a small fee or reciprocates another day. This setup gives her time to plug away at her novel, and her daughter is happily entertained. If you have a spare room in your house, you may be amazed to discover that you can hire an au pair for a small weekly fee in exchange for room and board. Many young women and men from around the world are eager to improve their English skills and gain a deeper understanding of another culture. I wouldn't have been able to write this book without the thirty hours of service I get each week from our lovely au pair from Childcare International. It isn't as expensive as you may think. We love ours, and she has become part of the family now.

One of my clients in London, a single mother of a five-year-old, was making slow progress in starting her own consulting business. She thought she should be able to do it and look after her daughter simultaneously, but instead her daughter felt ignored, while she felt frustrated at not being able to get enough work done. She hired an au pair, and that made all the difference. Her daughter was happy to have someone to play with after school, and my client was happy to be able to direct her attention to her business and support the family. In another case a friend of mine had an old garage converted into a small house for her mother and father; they take their grandchildren to and from school and also cover the after-school hours while she is busy fighting crime as a police detective. If you don't have the good fortune of family to help with child care, or space for an au pair, you may need to think outside the box.

Get creative. A retired neighbor does our ironing and mending once a week. A local student acts as a gal Friday and runs around doing office tasks and errands for us. If you plan on having a family and building a business, you need to delegate absolutely everything you possibly can. If you don't, you'll end up burning out, and both your business and—worse—your family will suffer, and you'll be miserable!

Eliminate or Reduce Your Commute

I once read somewhere that if your commute entails driving more than forty-five minutes each way, it is bad for your health and that it is worth moving closer to your work site or getting a job closer to your home. Now, with the advances in technology, more and more people can work effectively from home. If you can negotiate with your boss to work at least one or two days from home, this arrangement will save you not just your commute time but the time it takes to get dressed for work too. Make sure you are more productive on your home days, and let your boss see your results so that you can negotiate for even more time off-site. You'll be saving more time this way than would first appear. You will have fewer interruptions at home and will be incredulous at how much easier it is to get things done. As previously noted, you'll save time getting ready as well, since you don't need to worry about your appearance if no one is going to see you in your home office. Just avoid using video when talking to clients! Without all the office interruptions, you should be able to do your work in about half the span it would normally take, saving you anywhere from two to six hours a day. The more time you can trim from your current job, the more time you will have available to think about your ideal career, go on informational interviews, write your résumé, or start work on your own business.

Some jobs require your attendance (such as mine did at the bank), but that doesn't mean you can't use your time there more wisely.

I put my commute time to healthful and productive use by walking an hour a day both to and from work while listening to inspiring audio programs. You could also try biking. Use your lunch hour to develop new skills and/or contacts (I used mine to go to Toastmasters International to develop my speaking skills), and tap the resources of the company to get new training in your areas of interest. Be alert to all the opportunities around you to add to your skill base and gain experience in areas that appeal to you. Volunteer to take on projects that will get you exposure to different departments, fields, or industries. You may bump into the perfect business contact or job opportunity in the process. If nothing else, you will acquire skills and experience that will help you hone in on your ideal work. Even if you try something and discover that you don't like it, that is useful information and will help you narrow down your parameters. Use the resources around you to help you transition or build skills for your new career.

Career Transition: Important Things to Consider

In addition to carving out more time, it is also extremely helpful to have a financial cushion in place. It is ever so much easier to say, "Take this job and shove it!" if you have a solid two year's living expenses socked away. Statistically, most small businesses fail during the first two years of business because of lack of capital. If you don't want to become yet another statistic, take the time to get your own financial house in order. Reinventing your career might mean that you need to go back to school or get additional training. These things take time and can usually be done while

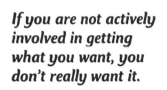

If you are not actively involved in getting what you want, you don't really want it.

—JOHN-ROGER AND PETER MCWILLIAMS

you are still holding down a job that covers your expenses. And it might make sense to experiment first to make sure you will actually enjoy doing it before you leave your current occupation.

Get Your Financial Reserve in Place

As much as I was hankering to quit my bank job so I could coach full-time, my first coach, Thom Politico, urged me to hang on to my day job until I had two years of living expenses in a money market account socked away and my credit card debts under control. This is wise counsel and is essential if you have a family to support.

Remember, most businesses fail in the first two years, not because they were poorly run or were bad ideas, but simply because the owner didn't have enough capital in place to ride out the inevitable ups and downs of a new business. At the time, I thought I'd never save enough, but once I started saving, I found I attracted money from unexpected sources. I received an unexpected bonus and promotion at the bank. Other clients have reported that money seems to appear once they start a savings plan—dividends from an investment they had long forgotten about, an inheritance from a distant relative, or an unexpected gift from a friend or family member.

If you recall Ali Brown's story, she quit her job with no savings, and it was extremely stressful as she worried how she would pay her bills. In hindsight, Ali wouldn't advise quitting without a solid reserve in place. There is no reason to put yourself through so much financial stress. You can build your business in your spare time while still keeping a job to pay the bills.

Again, more tips on this topic appear in *Coach Yourself to Success*. If you have debts, then pick up the extremely helpful book *How to Get Out of Debt, Stay Out of Debt, and Live Prosperously* by Jerrold Mundis. It was one of the best investments I have ever made. The more closely you stick to his plan, the sooner you'll be out of debt. Deviate from it and the process will just take longer, but you'll get there in the end. There are more helpful financial books and audio programs listed in the Resources and at Lifecoach.com.

Test the Waters Before You Transition

You may need to develop skills, get training, or pursue additional education to make the transition to your ideal career. And, if you are starting your own business, you may need to keep your day job (unless you already have at least two year's living expenses in reserve) and perform your business activities on evenings and weekends while you are getting under way. I did this when I started my coaching company. After a day at the bank, I'd come home, take a quick nap, and then start coaching. If you are currently employed, you can get a sense of a different industry or field that holds allure by going on informational interviews to learn more about a given company to which you might want to move. You can gain practical experience in that industry or field by doing volunteer work, by enrolling in evening classes, by taking on part-time or temporary work, and by joining the representative associations. I'm all for getting a toe wet first before diving in completely.

One client, Michaela, thought it would be really fun and glamorous to be a personal shopper for busy executives who didn't have the time to do their own shopping. Before quitting her day job in a retail shop, Michaela tried this out on some of her mother's friends, using her evenings and weekends to shop for them. She soon discovered it was a major

> *While one person hesitates because he feels inferior, the other is busy making mistakes and becoming superior.*
>
> —HENRY C. LINK

hassle dealing with the shipping and all the returns. In the end, she decided to stay in retail and got a job buying clothes for the store. She gets to go shopping, but on a much bigger scale! Sometimes things aren't as much of a hoot as they look on the surface, so field-test your ideas first any way you can.

Start Getting the Training and Experience You Need Now

If you are jumping from one field into a completely different field, you may need to go back to school full-time or take courses in the evening and on weekends. Your company may even have a training department in-house that offers relevant programs or may pay for you to take outside courses. For example, if you are in operations and want to switch into sales, you can probably take some in-house sales-training courses. It is easier to get the training at your current company and make the transition internally before you make the transition to another company. This is simply because with other candidates out there who have the relevant experience, your own résumé will look pretty weak in comparison.

You may need to go back to school to get a specific degree or type of training before you can change your field or career. Don't be afraid to do this, but make sure you have done enough informational interviews and values work to ensure that you are not wasting your time pursuing education that isn't necessary to your career or business success. I had one client, very briefly, who was dead set on getting an M.B.A. for the status of it, even though she wasn't a numbers person and would probably never want the sort of job that would require an M.B.A. Why waste all that money and time if you don't actually need the degree?

On the other hand, a client who was in her early sixties confessed to me that she had never been to college. I pointed out that nobody cared, since it hadn't affected her career, and that many very successful people dropped out of school (Bill Gates, for example). She still believed that she was missing out on something important and felt insecure around people who had been to college. She hesitated about going back to school, though, because of her age. My response was that she could go back to school and graduate and be sixty-six years old with a college degree, or she could postpone it and be sixty-six years old without a college degree: which did she prefer? She laughed and decided to go to school!

Use the informational interviews (see the discussion that follows) and do some research *before* you enroll in training programs and academic classes. The people who are already established in the field in which you are interested may have some viable suggestions on the best schools or training programs for that particular job or career, as well as on which ones to avoid.

Reinvent Your Networking and Interviewing Style

Now that you are equipped with your career profile and have outlined what you want to do, I thought it would also be helpful to give you a few networking and interviewing tips that will help you find the right job. You may have heard this said once or twice before: it's who you know that can help open new doors and opportunities for you. The number one way that people get jobs is through their friends, family, and contacts—not by sending out thousands of résumés or by submitting online applications through various career websites. So, here is what you need to do:

1. ***Get your elevator speech down pat.*** When asked what it is you want to do, you don't want to be caught off guard as I once was and left speechless or muttering something horribly vague about being a people person. Fortunately, after doing all the prior exercises, you should be pretty clear about what you want to do. Now the ticket is to take a few minutes to distill this goal into a maximum of three sentences. You might want to try this formula: "Hello, I'm _____ (your name). I love to _____ (thing you love doing) and am interested in exploring the field of _____ (fill in the blank). Do you know anyone in this field with whom I could have an informational interview?"

2. ***Have informal interviews with people, and ask, ask, ask questions.*** The rule is: Never ask for a job! When you ask someone for an informational interview, make it clear that you are not asking for a job, but are doing research on the field. When you are granted the chance to meet or to speak over the phone, just ask the person questions about the particular field. Most people love to talk about themselves and their work, especially if they are happy in their jobs. The following are some trusted openers:

   → What is the thing you love most about your work?
   → Describe a typical day.
   → Tell me how you got started in this industry/field/line of work.

   Be sure to ask anything you really want to know. Thank people for their time when you have finished, and follow up with a thank-you letter. In that letter, you might say something like this: "It was a pleasure speaking with you the other day. I really enjoyed hearing about XYZ and can see that you are passionate about what you do. You've helped me clarify my own career direction. Depending on your circumstances, you could add: "If you know of any openings in this field, I'd be grateful if you would pass on that information."

Thank you very much for your time. Sincerely yours, [signature]."
The more personal references you include about how the individual
has helped you in your career research, the better.

3. ***Make a list of all the people you know.*** Scan your entire circle of
   acquaintances to see if there is anyone already in the field or career
   you are targeting. If you succeed, call those people for informational
   interviews. Again, follow up with thank-you letters immediately. And
   in case you are wondering, *immediately* means mail the letter by
   no later than the morning after the interview. This shows you are
   prompt, professional, and thorough—and will separate you from
   those who don't follow up as quickly or at all. If no one you know
   is doing what you'd like to be doing, then just call people from
   your list who may know someone in that field and ask for a contact
   name and number. It may not be someone you know directly, but
   instead be just one person removed, who has the answers or the
   job you are seeking!

Reinvent Your Image—Dress for the Career You Want

When I quit my banking job, I decided I needed a new image to
go with my new coaching career. I wanted to be a life coach and
speak internationally about coaching. I interviewed three image
consultants in New York before hiring the one I thought was the
best, Carolyn Gustafson, who has since moved to Charlotte, North
Carolina. We discussed my objectives, and I explained that I still
wanted to look professional but didn't want to dress as conserva-
tively as a banker.

A little background: One of my female colleagues had been rep-
rimanded by the male manager for wearing leather boots instead
of pumps during the winter—he didn't think boots looked professional enough. When I was hoping to get laid off, I started wearing
pants on occasion and felt like a complete rebel. They didn't fire
me, though!

Carolyn came to my house and went through every single item
in my wardrobe and dresser. When she was done, I was left with

only two suits (one of them marginal) to get me started. I then had a designer tailor a new wardrobe for me, since I wasn't an off-the-shelf size—very few people are. I must have spent about $7,000 on this new wardrobe, which, given that I was recently unemployed and starting my own business, didn't seem like a very sound business decision, but what it gave me was worth every penny. I knew that I looked my best, and that gave me the confidence I needed. For example, when I was on TV as a guest, I wasn't one bit concerned about my appearance. I was able to focus all my attention and energy on the interviewer.

> *Don't be afraid to take a big step if one is indicated. You can't cross a chasm in two small jumps.*
>
> —DAVID LLOYD GEORGE

Having the right look is considerably more important than you may realize. If you feel self-conscious or worried about your appearance, all that angst will consume your precious energy. Remember to dress for the career or the work that you want, not the one you have.

When I was at Georgetown working on my master's degree, I had the opportunity to take a business class with one of the adjunct professors. He wasn't an academic but rather served as a vice president of the Import Export Bank. He told us that he expected us to wear our business suits to class, because when you go on an interview, you don't want to feel uncomfortable in your suit. For a student used to lounging around in a T-shirt and jeans, wearing a business suit felt strange at first, but it was valuable advice—wear the clothes that are appropriate to the career that you want. And practice wearing them before your interviews so they feel completely natural.

If you can afford it, I'd highly recommend working with an image consultant. The sooner you do this, the longer you'll reap the rewards, and the more money you'll save, because you'll know exactly what designers look best on you, what jacket is most flattering, which cuts and colors are best for you, even what sort of glasses, cosmetics, and hairstyle accentuate your best features. Knowing what works for your body type and coloring is well worth the initial investment in hiring an excellent image consultant. Also, as a side benefit, dressing for the career you want will help you attract that career as well. People who interview you or encounter you will immediately sense that you are "one of them." It is no good to show up for an advertising job wearing a conservative banker's suit unless you are applying to work in the accounting department! One of my senior executive banking clients mentioned she couldn't focus on an interview candidate because the young lady was snapping the string of her bikini. She clearly wasn't dressed appropriately for a banking job! Get a friend to make a video while you conduct a mock interview to ensure you aren't unconsciously making any distracting gestures or movements. It is all part of projecting the right image.

If getting an image consultant isn't in your budget right now, you can often get free fashion and style consultations from the better department stores. Many will provide you with a free personal shopper. Scout around until you find someone who really understands you and the look you want to achieve. When you've been on an informational interview or two, take note of the style changes you'd like to make so that you look the part for that field or job. Perhaps you have a friend with a keen sense of style who could go shopping with you and give you honest feedback. You can also find reliable resources about colors and styles that work best for you online and in books available for free at the local library.

Career Reinvention: Be Open to Change and New Experiences

Many people make the mistake of listening only to their heads instead of using their entire body to help them choose the right career path. A job can look great on paper, but if your heart isn't in it, then it isn't the right job for you. If you aren't jumping up and down with joy, then it may not be the right choice. That being said, some jobs are so new you'll have no way of knowing if it is right until you actually try it. Listen to the cues around you, to what your body and mind are trying to tell you, to your hopes as well as your fears, and you'll soon find the way.

Let Your Body Lead the Way

Now that you've learned several important factors to weigh during your career transition, such as the status of your financial reserves and the skill set you'll need, other pertinent considerations should be addressed, including what your body is telling you and what the cues around you indicate. It always behooves you to listen to your body—your body gives you signals about how you really feel about your current job or career.

Returning to an earlier example, when I was working at Chase managing a financial center in downtown Manhattan, I used to walk the hour it took to get to work instead of riding the subway. I figured that it supposedly took only thirty minutes on the subway, but if the train got stuck somewhere, it would take about forty-five minutes, so I had to realistically allocate forty-five minutes commuting time. Thus, for an extra fifteen minutes, I traded the rather unpleasant experience of being squeezed into a hot and sweaty train for a brisk and beneficial hour-long walk. This was my built-in exercise program as well, and it kept me fit. However, this entire time, my body was telling me that it didn't want me to go to work. I would be walking along, and all of the sudden my back would seize up, and I wouldn't be able to take a step. As the problem persisted, I went to a chiropractor for treatment two to three times a week. My body was trying to stop me from going to work at the bank, but I went on slogging it out while saving up money so I could quit with two years' reserve in place.

> *My grandmother started walking five miles a day when she was sixty. She's ninety-five now, and we don't know where the hell she is.*
>
> —ELLEN DEGENERES

Funny thing, the day I quit my job was the day my back spasms ended!

What is your body trying to tell you? The message will keep getting louder and louder (i.e., more and more painful) until you listen up. One of my clients was experiencing numbness in her limbs. She hated her job, but it paid so well that she couldn't bring herself to quit. The most dramatic example I've ever encountered along these lines was a client who had an alarming pattern in her life. I usually ask my clients to write down their life stories for me before our first coaching call, so that I can quickly get the lay of the land and form a sense of who they are and what they've already accomplished. When I read her story, I was stunned to see that she had a history of going out with a guy, getting in an accident and breaking some part of her body (such as an arm or a leg), and then breaking up with the guy. She didn't spot the pattern herself until she wrote down her life story, and then she was horrified to realize that she felt she had to break a part of her body before she could muster the courage to break up with the guy!

Your body is, in many ways, much wiser than your head. It knows what the right path in life is for you. When I'm working with clients and they discuss the options that lie in front of them, I can tell by their tone of voice which is the one that they are most excited about. It isn't rocket science. Listen to your body. What does it really want to do right now?

When you are on the right path, a whole host of physical complaints may suddenly disappear. That is a good clue that you are doing the work and leading the life you are meant to have. If you are riddled with odd aches and pains, then listen up, because you probably aren't headed in the right direction. That's when you know it's time for a change!

Listen to the Cues Around You

Another way to determine whether you're heading in the right direction in terms of your career path is to listen to the subtle cues around you. You may be familiar with the old childhood game called "hot and cold." In my family's version, every year at Easter our bunny would hide pennies all over the house as well as an Easter basket for my sisters and me. If hours passed and we still couldn't find our basket, our parents would play "hot and cold" with us. The farther away from the basket we walked, the "cooler" it got, and my parents would say, "You are getting cold now . . . you are starting to freeze." As we turned in the right direction, it was, "You are getting warm . . . now you are getting really warm . . . you are boiling!" That's how we found the basket.

> *In no other period of history were the learned so mistrustful of the divine possibilities in man as they are now.*
>
> —GOPI KRISHNA

Get in the habit of taking cues from your present circumstances—kind of like playing this "hot and cold" game. If you are miserable and catch yourself having random negative thoughts, such as that getting hit by a bus and spending a month in traction would be preferable to going to your job, essentially this cue is telling you that you are on the wrong path in life. Alternatively, when you are on the right path, things start to heat up: your pulse beats a little faster, you feel excited, your ears prick up—that is a good sign that you are pointed toward the right target! And once you find your metaphorical "basket," you can sit down and enjoy the contents. Life gets much easier when we are on the right path!

Reinvent Your Fears—Facing Uncertainty Can Lead to Your Plan B

If you have been following the steps in this program, you won't really have a huge issue with fear, but your lingering fear of change and lifestyle shifts during this transition time can still affect your decision making. I remember once a seminar leader asked everyone in the room who didn't love his or her work to stand up. At the time, I was working at the bank, so I stood up right away along with a bevy of others. Then he challenged us: "Quit your job today and do something you love instead." I broke into a cold, nervous sweat then and there. Fear and panic were my immediate reactions. And rightly so. I was up to my eyeballs in credit card debt, I was living in Manhattan and was locked into a lease on an apartment at a high rent, and I had no idea what I wanted to do when I grew up other than that I knew it wasn't banking! As much as I wanted to quit, I was in no position to do so. And if you've got kids and a mortgage, no wonder the hair is standing straight up on the back of your neck! Fear is our friend. It tells us when we are about to be eaten by a bear or about to fall off a cliff. Pay attention to it!

> *Do the thing you fear, and the death of fear is certain.*
>
> —RALPH WALDO EMERSON

One easy way to overcome your fears is to fully understand them. Take a few minutes to examine your fears and think about what exactly you are afraid of. Write these things down. Imagine the worst-case scenario: If you were to quit your job, what is the worst possible thing that could happen? Is this scenario valid, or are you just being dramatic? In other words, would you really be a bag lady on the streets, or do you actually have a number of friends and family members you could live with while you sort out your life?

Most fears miraculously diminish in proportion to the amount of funds we have saved in reserve. The more money you have saved, the less fear you harbor. You literally can *afford* to take the risk. You know you have the reserves to get through a rough patch or two, so you aren't afraid to try something new, whether that is starting a business or switching careers. Then again, this isn't always the case.

I've mentioned before, my client Melissa Todd, the owner of Hip Hounds, was afraid of giving up her steady income at the law firm. Fear was one of the forces that prevented her from quitting and working on her business full-time. She admitted that she actually had the money saved but worried that it wasn't enough. It wasn't until the clash between her core values and the firm's values became glaringly obvious that she finally made the leap and quit her job to work on her business full-time—a bold move in the middle of one of the worst recessions since the Great Depression. Her father thought she was crazy to give up the security of her job. Melissa thought about her fears, and in her worst-case scenario—her business goes bust—she knew that she could always get another legal job. She carefully considered her fears and realized that since her worst-case scenario wasn't actually that bad, she could in fact quit. She finally realized she had more to lose by staying in her job than by quitting and devoting her full attention to growing Hip Hounds. Her business, which most experts would consider a luxury service (a high-end dog day care and boarding facility), grew 15 percent during a terrible recession! Just goes to show you how much value people place on taking good care of their pets!

It is worth spending some time finding ways to reduce or eliminate your fears. If you are afraid you won't have enough money, start saving 50 percent of your income by cutting your expenses ruthlessly. Pay off all your debts, line up your disability insurance while you are still employed, and make sure you have two years of living expenses in a savings or money market account before you hand in your resignation. It also helps to have a plan B in the event that things don't work out according to plan A. My plan B for quitting was asking the manager of a local Italian restaurant if he would hire me to be a hostess if I needed some extra money while I built my coaching company. He said he would. At one point, he asked me if I would come in and work, but I was too busy coaching!

If you are worried about not being able to pay the rent or mortgage, it may be good to ask your friends and family members if they would be willing to accommodate you in the event of disaster. Just knowing you have a welcome place to go can alleviate a lot of unnecessary fear.

If you are scared you don't have the talent to be successful, you can always invest a small amount of time and money in taking various computerized assessments to find out if your talents align with the kind of career you'd like to explore (take a look at the Resources section for more information). Another option is to start what you want to be doing in the evenings and on weekends to develop your talent or skill. Take courses, classes, or seminars that can add to your foundation. These preliminary activities can also give you a firmer sense of whether you would enjoy switching jobs or careers!

You may still be wondering if what I've been telling you from square one is really possible: can you actually find the ideal career or start your own business in your spare time? The answer is a resounding, "Absolutely, yes!"

SUCCESS STORY

The Student Who Graduated and Started Her Own Charity

Quinn Simpson is a cofounder of Akosia.org, a project to create a summer program for street children in Ghana. She is also the founder of the Stepping Up Program, which coaches sixteen- to twenty-four-year-olds, and is a coach as well. She herself is twenty-four years old and is unstoppable now that she has found her real passion in life. Quinn originally thought she wanted to be a photographer. Photography was her passion; she was great at it, loved it, and was certain it would become her career. She took a job shooting still photographs on a TV show, and in one week she knew it wasn't enough for her—she realized she needed to help people. The only way she knew that her initial choice was wrong was by trying it.

After her experience behind the camera, she concluded that she was supposed to become a social worker and was convinced that was the career for her. She studied social work in college and, during that time, started working with very poor families in Scotland. It depressed her—not just the poverty but also the knowledge that no matter what she did, it wasn't enough. She dropped her social work studies, and in her third year of college she focused on anthropology and sociology instead—not really knowing what she would do. It wasn't until her fourth year, when her mother sent her *Coach Yourself to Success* and she took my seminars and phone classes, that she started to think that coaching would be the career for her. As soon as she graduated, she enrolled in not one, but two, of the best coach-training programs and is now coaching young people to find their passion in life and working with African street children to create a movie. Her vision is to bring coaching into education, and her big future goal is to become a talk-show host on TV. I fully believe that she'll do it.

Quinn never waits for the future and instead does what she wants to do now. If it doesn't work out, she tries something else. Sometimes it has been difficult. She was coaching from nine to five in London and then looking after an elderly disabled man in the evenings in order to cover living expenses. Her life has been a process of experimentation, and as a result, she has found her passion in life at a very young age and has already started three businesses that she loves.

Talane interviews her client, Quinn:

What was the shift for you?

Something you said in the Coach Yourself to Success *phone class has stuck with me: "You have to give yourself the life you want before you have it." You suggested starting with something as simple as hiring a house cleaner before you are rich. Living the future that you want now.*

What was the best outcome from your career transition?

I love Mondays! I have no idea what opportunities and people will come in a week. I make my week happen. I decide what happens. And I love coaching! I'm filled up with energy after a coaching call. I love my life, and I love being me.

How did you overcome your fear of change?

I'm a risk taker. At eleven years old, I realized that I wasn't "cool" because I was trying to be like everyone else. I stopped trying to be like everyone else, and I became "cool," and suddenly everyone wanted to be my friend. Stop worrying so much about what other people think or about what is going to happen. We are all afraid of something: get over it. You have only one chance. Life is precious. You can be afraid. Take a step. Dip your toe into the outside of your comfort zone. Treat your scary, uncomfortable place like a pool, and slowly work your way into it. Don't get out; stay in it. I didn't start out being a good networker. I was a bit scared going in and didn't know what I was doing. You'll never know unless you try. Just stick a toe in.

What personal advice would you like to give others who also want to transition in their careers?

I genuinely believe that everyone has a purpose, a unique talent. Everyone has a dream; even if it is buried, it's there. The only way to find it is to spend time looking for it. I spent hours thinking about who I am. I was always reflecting on experiences. So many of us look outside of ourselves for the answer. We need to look within ourselves. You already know it. Ask yourself, "What is my dream?"

Bonus Tips for Career Success

Using a Little Magic

Make no little plans: they have no magic to stir men's blood.

—DANIEL HUDSON BURNHAM

Now that you are armed with a seven-step program for a successful career transition, I'd like to offer some extra tips and tricks to you. I've found that it never hurts to use a little magic to make things happen faster. Again, this stuff may sound a bit out-there, but there is documented evidence both in my life and in the lives of numerous clients that these tricks work! You don't have to believe that they will work for them to work, so why not have a go at them just for fun and see what happens? They require very little on your part in terms of time or money, so you have essentially nothing to lose and everything to gain.

> *Fortune sides with him who dares.*
>
> —VIRGIL

Feng Shui Tips for Career Success

If you are feeling stuck in a rut or trapped in a job that you don't particularly like, are unemployed and looking for work, or are eager to advance in your current career, then you may want to do a few little feng shui experiments. One of my favorite books on this topic is *Move Your Stuff, Change Your Life* by Karen Rauch Carter. I'm a proponent of applying simple feng shui techniques after being highly skeptical initially. Here are a few tips from feng shui to help boost your career possibilities—keep in mind that these nuggets do not do justice to this ancient art, but they fill the bill as some basic starting points:

→ **Make sure your desk faces the door but isn't in direct line with it.** You never want your back toward the door. You need to be able to look up and see who is coming into your office, but at the same time, you don't want your desk to be directly in front of the door. Just make sure that you can look up and see who is coming in. If you have a cubicle, the same principles apply. If you can't have your desk face the cubicle entrance, then try to make sure you can work from the side, so you can see who is coming. If this is impossible, then hang a small mirror or something else reflective so you can see who is approaching behind you. Do this at your home office as well as at work.

→ **Put your bookshelves (ideally wooden) behind your desk to either side of your chair so that you are flanked on both sides by books.** This arrangement lends authority and respect automatically. You may think it's foolish, as I did at first, but the effects of feng shui are both subtle and powerful. I wish I had known about this tip when I was pitching my first book, *Coach Yourself to Success*, to a big New York publisher. I was the second person to walk into a conference room that had a large round table in the middle, and I was offered first choice of chairs. There was a wall of bookcases on one side and a wall of glass on the other side. Instinctively, I didn't take a seat with my back to the door, mainly because that would have been awkward as more people entered the room. After a moment's indecision, I sat with my back to the window, which overlooked Manhattan. Although I gave a dynamite pitch to the publishing team and felt entirely positive about it, when my agent called me, she said they liked the coaching concept but didn't think I had enough authority and credibility. I'll wager that if I had sat with my back against the wall of books, which would have lent some authority, I would have sealed the deal. These subtle touches can make the difference between getting a job and not getting one.

→ **Right behind your chair, hang a beautiful picture or piece of artwork.** This image may be something you find beautiful, inspiring, or peaceful. It will welcome you to the office every time you enter, and it will also bring an element of your personal taste and style to the work setting. Make sure it is a piece of art that would garner respect if you would like to win respect. The picture will reflect on you, so be certain it is making the statement you want.

→ **The main entry to your home is usually associated with your career.** Do you use the main door of your residence, or do you always use a side or back door? If the latter is the case, this habit may mirror how you are always being overlooked for promotions or jobs. Try using your front door for a change. One of my clients did this and discovered that he couldn't open the front door from the outside without grazing a knuckle—it had the wrong sort of knob. No wonder "doors of opportunity" weren't opening easily for him at work. He changed his door handle and a few days later was invited to host his own radio show—something he had always dreamed of doing but didn't know how to make happen.

→ **Make sure your front entrance reflects authority as well as being welcoming and tidy.** Remove any obstacles to the entryway. Verify that the front door opens and closes easily without obstruction and that it doesn't stick. Check that the doorbell works and there is plenty of light. If you have a double front door, take care not to block one of the doors with a potted plant or statue, or you'll be blocking half your chi (good energy).

→ **Use symbols and figurines if you feel you need protection from toxic colleagues or bosses.** Add a pair of concrete figurines of dogs or lions symbolically guarding the front door of your home, and paint the door red (red is the color of protection). These feng shui cures for the home can serve to protect you at work as well, as it may be neither possible nor practical to deploy two concrete lions to guard your cubicle entrance!

→ **Add a water element.** Hang a mirror somewhere in the front entryway. Mirrors represent water, and water is helpful for career success. This is why you typically see an aquarium with fish when you enter a Chinese restaurant. Glass, water, and the movement of the fish all promote positive energy. A glass vase of water with some flowers also works, or even silk flowers with plastic water as representation of a water element.

→ **Be careful what pictures or paintings you hang at your home's entrance.** The images you display should represent what you want, not what you don't want. I had a client who was married and lived in a beautiful apartment in Amsterdam. Hanging to the immediate left of their apartment door was a shocking Salvador Dalí print depicting a tiger about to devour a naked woman. The fact that the artist was famous did not offset the sheer violence of the scene. I later found out that they had a very unsatisfying personal life along with constant career troubles. I'm not surprised given the subject matter of the print and its location near the career area of their home.

→ **Get rid of clutter at home and at work.** I've emphasized this concept in previous chapters because it's critical to your professional success! In the world of feng shui, clutter represents stuck energy. So, if you feel mired at work or in a job you don't like, then get busy clearing the clutter! Start with your front entrance and work your way around the house room by room. If that seems overwhelming, grab a shopping bag and, every day, put six things into it that you can readily get rid of, and then drop the bag off at your favorite charity. Do this for one week. You'll soon be unstuck and on your way to a successful career. In fact, some clients find that as soon as they clear the clutter, they end up attracting a great job and don't even have to do the rest of the exercises in the program.

These tips apply whether you live in a house, an apartment, or some other type of domicile. I know that the whole concept of feng shui sounds wacky to the Westerner, but the way I figure it is that the techniques are easy and relatively inexpensive to implement, so why not take a shot? If they work, you win. If not, you've lost nothing. If nothing else, consider the implementation of these tips a powerful ritual that will enhance your career success. The art of feng shui has been practiced for more than two thousand years in Eastern countries, and the concept is growing more and more popular worldwide, so there's certainly *something* going on there!

Write It Down and Make It Happen

If this tip sounds vaguely familiar, you might have read it in *Coach Yourself to Success*, but it is so potent that it bears revisiting here. There is an inspiring book called *Write It Down, Make It Happen* by Henriette Anne Klauser, in which she documents with one compelling story after another the powerful impact of simply writing down what you want. There is tremendous power in taking hold of an ephemeral thought and writing it down. It is the first step in making the transition to what you really want—bringing your wishes, hopes, and dreams out of the world of fancy and into the world of reality. The moment your thoughts are written down, they take on a life of their own. No longer something inside you, your thoughts now exist in the physical realm. You can read them, see them, and touch the paper containing your written words.

> *Every man has one thing he can do better than anyone else and usually that is reading his own handwriting.*
>
> —G. NORMAN COLLIE

A brilliant thought may come as a sudden insight and be gone in an instant, but if you take a moment to write it down, it will be captured, not lost. Profound insights may come in a flash when you are taking a shower, just as you are going to bed at night, or while you're commuting to work. Get in the habit of keeping a pen and pad by your bed, as well as in your purse or briefcase or in your car, so that when you have an intriguing idea, you can note it. Some of my clients prefer to carry a small recording device instead and record their thoughts as they occur to them. Whatever works best for you.

In addition to jotting down good ideas, you can use the power of writing things down to achieve specific goals or wishes. It works best to focus on one major goal or dream at a time. This keeps you from diluting your energy by working on too many goals or projects at a clip. Once you've decided which has priority, write it down fifteen times a day until it comes true. Here's how to do it: Write your specific goal or objective in the present tense, and start your sentence with "I am [fill in the blank]." So, instead of writing, "I will be earning $150,000 on September 22, 2010," write, "I am earning $150,000 a year as a [fill in the blank]." If you are not getting what you want, it may be that it isn't in your best interest or in the best interest of all concerned. For example, it would not be wise to wish your competitors or your boss dead. Keep your thoughts and goals completely positive. Negative thoughts boomerang back to you with negative results. Who would you like to be? Write down your biggest "I am" statement fifteen times a day, and the genie of the universe will go to work.

> *I was going to buy a copy of The Power of Positive Thinking, and then I thought: "What the hell good would that do?"*
>
> —RONNIE SHAKES

This is also an extremely effective technique to use before asking for a pay increase, raising your client rates in your business, or negotiating a salary-and-benefits package at a new company. One of my senior-executive clients, Catherine, used this technique before negotiating her compensation at another company. I told her that she shouldn't accept the job offer until she was literally jumping up and down with glee. The current offer was pretty good, but it just wasn't enough to get her excited. I could hear in her voice that she had some reservations about taking the job at that rate. I asked Catherine to make a list of all the things she wanted in the new job: what base salary, bonuses, benefits, perks, and so on. She took some time to think this over carefully and then wrote down everything she could possibly think of. Then Catherine wrote down, "I am making $_ a year at XYZ company" over and over until it sounded perfectly reasonable to her. With enough repetition, you actually program your brain into believing that your statement is true and possible. If you don't believe it can happen, then it probably won't!

Catherine could then go back to the people recruiting her and tell them point by point what would make her leave her current company. She was able to ask for what she wanted (and it was a lot!) with calm, cool confidence. She knew that if she hadn't thought it through, she would have been tempted to take the lower offer. By writing it down, she was able to clarify her wishes. She said if she hadn't done this preparatory work, she would not have had the calm assurance and boldness to ask for what she wanted. And wouldn't you know: she got what she wanted! As a general rule, always ask for more than you think you deserve.

The reason for writing your wish down fifteen times a day is to beat it into your brain until you actually start believing it is true. Be aware that the first time you write the words, all those little voices in your head will start chiding, "Who do you think you are anyway to ask for that much money? You'll never get this. Who are you kidding? No one gets that much vacation time." Keep on writing and eventually you'll get to the point where those little voices will be saying, "Sure, you can get this. Piece of cake. What's the big deal?" That's when you know you've made the necessary mental shift from wanting to having. Get out your pen and start putting the power of writing it down to work!

Creative Visualization

Creative visualization is a simple technique popularized by Shatki Gawain in her book of the same title. Having positive thoughts is an aid to achieving your goal, be it a new career, a dream job, or success in any other venture. It helps to imagine what you *want* to have happen, rather than what you don't want to have happen. I was coaching a bright, industrious twenty-something woman who was working for the United Nations and was asked by her boss to give a presentation to about a hundred people from different countries. She had never given a presentation before and was justifiably terrified. Most people are more afraid of public speaking than they are of death—not rational, but true nevertheless! As she prepared for her presentation, she kept imagining all of the horrible scenarios that could happen, such as blanking out, not being able to speak, and even fainting on the platform. I told her that it would be much better if

> *Imagination is more important than knowledge.*
>
> —ALBERT EINSTEIN

she acted those fears out in front of some friends and family to get them out of her system. Her assignment was to act out her worst fears while delivering her presentation. I wanted her to discover that you can drop your notes, faint, and blank out and still get up and carry on with your talk. Doing the practice talk in front of friends helped her overcome her major anxieties.

> *No man that does not see visions will ever realize any high hope or undertake any high enterprise.*
>
> —WOODROW WILSON

Then we worked on doing positive visualization instead. If she caught herself thinking of something negative, she was to just say, "Cancel, cancel" and then imagine the positive result she wanted: people coming up afterward to compliment her on the great presentation. She did this, and—just as she had envisioned—she did a great job and got compliments from her audience. Use the power of your mind to imagine the results you want and you'll very likely get them.

Have a Bit of Fun

Let's imagine that there are two service providers bidding for one job. The two are equally qualified. One of them is regularly doing something that he or she loves to do—whether that is waterskiing, kite boarding, ballroom dancing, knitting, or playing basketball. The other has cut out all such fun activities because there is a recession; being unemployed, this candidate has chosen to save as much money as possible and use all available free time to hunt for a new business. Which candidate will get the contract? The one having all the fun. I know this doesn't sound fair, but we can't help but be more attracted to the people who are out there enjoying life. They come across as being more enjoyable to be around, more relaxed, more energetic, and more fun than others. Who wouldn't want to work with someone who displays these qualities? If you own a business, the same applies to attracting clients. No one will want to do business with you if you are stressed-out and exhausted.

This doesn't mean you should be racking up credit card debt and living irresponsibly or dangerously, but it does mean that to find the ideal work or business, it is important to be regularly engaged in an activity that lights you up, makes you feel alive and wonderful, and energizes you. If you aren't already having some fun, now is definitely the time!

Programming Your Brain for Success

Scientists say we are using only a small percentage of our brains—as little as 10 percent. I firmly advocate using tools to tap into the other 90 percent. And why not leverage the subconscious power of the brain as long as you know those tools are safe? No purple Kool-Aid brainwashing, thank you very much! In addition to using creative visualization and writing down, "I am . . ." fifteen times a day (both are ways to consciously program your brain to focus on your goals), try using both paraliminal and subliminal audio programs for extra support.

Paraliminal programs feature positive suggestions or statements that you listen to while in a relaxed or semihypnotic state. You can hear every word that is spoken and should not be doing other tasks or activities during the session. These programs offer an easy way to meditate if you have difficulty meditating on your own or find your mind wanders. They are, in effect, guided meditations. *Subliminal* audio programs have hidden messages or statements that you can't hear at a conscious level. The message is usually buried under the pleasant and relaxing sounds of waves crashing on a beach or a babbling stream. A chief benefit of subliminal

> *Success is simply a matter of luck. Ask any failure.*
>
> —EARL WILSON

audio programs is that they can be played in the background while you are busy doing other tasks, as they don't interfere, and no one will know that you are actually filling your brain with positive messages while you are at the computer or the ironing board.

> *It matters not whether you win or lose; what matters is whether I win or lose.*
>
> —DARIN WEINBERG

When I started building my coaching business in New York, I played a subliminal program, *Attracting Infinite Riches* from Alphasonics International, while I was coaching clients or cooking dinner. It has a relaxing sound of a softly babbling brook. I kept it fairly low so that it was white noise and set my tape player on auto-repeat. When a friend came to visit, he commented on how relaxing the room was and mused that for some reason, the sound of the traffic in the background sounded like a stream. I clued him in to the fact that I had a tape on! Not only did this audio mask the traffic noise, but also it worked: I started attracting more clients, and my business grew rapidly. Please keep in mind that you must be very, very careful about subliminal programs and really trust the people who made them. It is all too easy to inadvertently plant a negative message. There should be no negative messages or statements whatsoever in a paraliminal or subliminal audio program. I was pleased to discover, after using the Alphasonics International subliminals for years, that one of my clients had worked with the creators and could vouch for them as gifted and excellent people and professionals. I've since been recommending these subliminal programs to my clients.

Recently I've discovered some wonderful paraliminal audio programs from Paul Scheele, which, as mentioned previously, work the other way around. You can hear the message in paraliminals, and the music is in the background. I use these as a way to do a guided meditation and pick whatever topic I need at the time, from health to success. In addition to being a great way to start meditating, these programs can be used to refresh yourself in the afternoon or after a busy day at work. Much better than a cup of coffee if you need a pick-me-up!

You can use both paraliminal and subliminal audio programs to work on any number of areas in your life (such as career, wealth, health, success, relationships, addictions), but it is best to focus on one area at a time. People who meditate regularly typically report that they get better and more creative ideas as a result. It is like tapping into a greater intelligence or wisdom. I've personally noticed that I get new ideas after listening to Paul Scheele's *Personal Genius* paraliminal audio program in the evening before bed. On one occasion, I awoke the next morning with a brilliant and admittedly obvious idea on how to become virtually mortgage free in one year. We are in the midst of doing this now, so I'll keep you posted as to how it works on my blog at Lifecoach.com. For more information about these paraliminal and subliminal audio programs, please see the "Resources" section, which follows this chapter, or use the Resources link on Lifecoach.com.

It's Time to Coach Yourself!

If you are like most people, you have read the book but haven't actually done any of the coaching assignments. This is normal and, actually, just fine. I always like to get a feel for a program first before embarking on the actions. Now go back and work through the seven steps of the program! If you don't do anything or make any changes, you have no right to expect your life to change. The danger in reading any self-help book is thinking you've actually done something. This book is all about taking action. Use it to coach yourself to a new career, business, or venture. I've made each of the seven steps as simple and easy as possible. Now it is up to you to take the action. Find a buddy or coach, or sign up for the online coaching program (you can find all three at Lifecoach.com), and start working through the steps.

> *Act as if it were impossible to fail.*
>
> —DOROTHEA BRANDE

There is a natural order to the program, but if you feel inspired to do a particular tip or step, go right ahead. Any action is better than no action! Beware, though, of the common desire to skip Step 2. It is perfectly natural and normal to want to bypass this step, because assessing our personal requirements is hard work. At the very minimum, allot twenty minutes to go online at Lifecoach.com and take the Personal Requirements Quiz there; then jot down your answers in your career profile in Step 6. Knowing what you need is indispensable to finding the ideal career or business and attracting the best people and opportunities. If you avoid Step 2, you risk being like the CEO who at the end of a successful and lucrative career realized that he still wasn't satisfied. That rankling discontent usually indicates that you haven't identified your personal requirements! It may not make sense to you now, but once you've done the work, it will seem a natural part of your life to ask directly for what you need and want.

> *Action is the antidote to despair.*
>
> —JOAN BAEZ

Shortcut to Coaching Yourself to a New Career

I'm a big fan of doing the least possible amount of work to get the result you want. So, I'm going to suggest a possible shortcut to this program. I've outlined the full career-coaching program in this book because many people need to take each and every one of these seven steps before they become clear on a new career path. Also, all of these steps will make you a happier and more successful person in general, which is always a good thing. That being said, some

> *He who hesitates is a damned fool.*
>
> —MAE WEST

of my clients take just a few of these steps and get the careers or businesses they want, so you may not have to do them all. As I mentioned in Step 1, I've had clients who just do a bit of clutter clearing and attract a great job almost instantly. If, at the close of this book, you feel a strong inclination to do a particular step right away, go ahead and do it, wherever it appears in the formal sequence. I'm also a big fan of following one's natural inclinations!

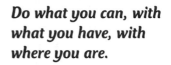

Do what you can, with what you have, with where you are.

—THEODORE ROOSEVELT

If you want a handy shortcut, here is a good one to try:

1. Take the Personal Requirements Quiz in Step 2. Write down your top four personal requirements in Step 6. (This will take about twenty minutes.)
2. Now go to Step 5 and do the work on your values and passions. Write down your top four to ten values in Step 6.
3. Now do the envy exercise in Step 5. If there is one single, most powerful assignment for identifying what it is you should do, this is it. Envy is pointing the way to what you really want. By carefully examining your envy, you can quickly identify the right career path. Use your envy as your guide. In fact, the Envy Method could be the whole book, except for the problem that most people don't believe they can go for what they envy until they've done all the other steps. So, go figure. Follow that green-eyed monster and you'll not only eliminate your envy but also have the career or business of your dreams.

There is one caveat: you need to do the personal requirements and values work first so that you can be sure that your envy is honest. You'll never go wrong by orienting your work and life around your values (Step 5), but you can go very, very wrong by orienting your work around the pursuit of money or that neighbor's new Porsche. Remember the example of Melissa Todd, who spent the first forty-some years of her life pursuing the wrong career at a big law firm (Step 6). It is perfectly natural to envy someone for being rich because you want to be able to enjoy that same fancy lifestyle, but when you get past wanting the trappings of success—those Chanel sunglasses or the spiffy car—then you know you've reached the heart of what will make you happy in work and in life. I guarantee you, it won't be the sunglasses!

> *Things may come to those who wait, but only the things left by those who hustle.*
>
> —ABRAHAM LINCOLN

If you do these three steps and still aren't sure what to do with your career, then go back and work through the full seven-step program from the beginning. As I said, all of these exercises are designed to help you find the ideal new career or venture, and all of them have the wonderful side benefit of making you a happier, more aware human being. Take even the tiniest of steps in the right direction—clear out a closet, sign up for a class that sounds exciting or interesting, compose an ideal job description, do something you'd do if you were a millionaire and money was no object—and things will start to shift and change before you know it. Above all, enjoy the process!

> *It is common sense to take a method and try it. If it fails, admit it frankly and try another. But above all, try something.*
>
> —FRANKLIN D. ROOSEVELT

I would love to hear how these steps helped you to find a new career or start a new business or venture. Please e-mail me at talane@lifecoach.com with your stories and comments. Thank you!

Resources

Additional Reading

Bolles, Richard Nelson. *What Color Is Your Parachute?* Berkeley, California: Ten Speed Press, 2009. A comprehensive manual for getting you through the career-change and interview process. A useful resource book updated every year.

Buckingham, Marcus, and Donald O. Clifton. *Now, Discover Your Strengths.* New York: The Free Press, 2001. The book contains an online strengths assessment that takes about twenty minutes to complete and will then tell you your top five strengths. Buy it new, as you want to be able to use the onetime password to access the assessment.

Edwards, Paul, and Sarah Edwards. *Finding Your Perfect Work: The New Career Guide to Making a Living and Creating a Life.* New York: Jeremy P. Tarcher/Putnam, 1996. A comprehensive and very useful manual.

Ferriss, Timothy. *The 4-Hour Workweek: Escape the 9–5, Live Anywhere, and Join the New Rich.* New York: Crown Publishers, 2007. An inspiring read with practical steps on starting your own business while still working full-time.

Gladwell, Malcolm. *Outliers: The Story of Success.* London: Penguin Books, 2008. Gladwell tells fascinating stories of what it really takes to be wildly successful in business.

Glassman, Bernard, and Rick Fields. *Instructions to the Cook: A Zen Master's Lessons in Living a Life That Matters.* New York: Bell Tower, 1997. If you lack the motivation to start work on your own special project, this little book will inspire you. You will learn to use what you have and recognize your faults as your best ingredients.

Greaves, Suzy. *Making the Big Leap: Coach Yourself to Create the Life You Really Want.* London: New Holland Publishers, 2007. If you are struggling with fear and want to quit and start your own business, read this inspiring little book written by one of my coaching colleagues in the UK.

Jones, Laurie Beth. *The Path: Creating Your Mission Statement for Work and for Life.* New York: Hyperion, 1996. A step-by-step process for creating a mission statement for your life that can be used to initiate, evaluate, and refine all of life's activities. Excellent questions to answer to create your own life plan.

Klauser, Henriette Anne. *Write It Down, Make It Happen: Knowing What You Want—and Getting It!* New York: Simon & Schuster, 2000. A fun read that will inspire you to start writing down exactly what you want.

Maslow, Abraham H. *Toward a Psychology of Being.* 2nd ed. New York: D. Van Nostrand Company, 1968. The original academic source for the hierarchy of needs; the concept that emotional needs are requirements for our self-actualization and well-being comes from Maslow. Read this to understand his early work on needs and their critical role in the process of human growth, development, and self-actualization. Also by Maslow is *Religions, Values, and Peak-Experiences.* New York: Penguin Compass, 1964.

McDonald, Bob, and Don E. Hutcheson. *Don't Waste Your Talent: The Eight Critical Steps to Discovering What You Do Best.* New York: The Highlands Company, 2005. The book describes in detail the results from The Highlands Program, the computerized online assessment that we use in Talane Coaching Company to help people identify their hardwired talents and abilities. This is the most comprehensive assessment that I currently know of on the market and the one we always recommend that anyone in career transition use to quickly identify his or her abilities.

Miedaner, Talane. *Coach Yourself to Success: 101 Tips from a Personal Coach for Reaching Your Goals at Work and in Life.* New York: Contemporary Books, 2000. My first book is full of simple yet powerful coaching tips to make you more successful in all areas of life, including how to create more money, time, space, and energy. If you are struggling to get your life on track, you might want to start with this book and then move on to my second book, *The Secret Laws of Attraction: The Effortless Way to Get the Relationship You Want,* which goes into great depth on personal and emotional needs and requirements. This book will help you get both the business and personal relationships you want and will improve your existing relationships as well.

Rauch Carter, Karen. *Move Your Stuff, Change Your Life: How to Use Feng Shui to Get Love, Money, Respect, and Happiness.* New York: Simon & Schuster, 2000. My all-time favorite book about feng shui. Fun to read, with easy steps on how to apply the feng shui principles to your home and office.

St. James, Elaine. *Simplify Your Life: 100 Ways to Slow Down and Enjoy the Things That Really Matter.* New York: Hyperion, 1994. A classic little book that will help you simplify your life so you have time to figure out your new, ideal career.

Smith, Manuel J. *When I Say No, I Feel Guilty.* New York: Bantam Books, 1975. If you say yes more often than you should, read this classic for some straightforward guidelines to end the doormat syndrome once and for all.

Tieger, Paul D., and Barbara Barron-Tieger. *Do What You Are: Discover the Perfect Career for You Through the Secrets of Personality Type.* Boston: Little Brown and Company, 1992. This book uses the Myers-Briggs Type Indicator (MBTI) to help you identify your personality type and your natural strengths and then suggests possible careers that match. This will help you strengthen your strengths and give up struggling.

Assessments

The Personal Requirements Quiz (Lifecoach.com)

To take the Personal Requirements Quiz, please go to the Free Stuff button on Lifecoach.com. The quiz takes about twenty minutes to complete, and you will instantly receive your top four personal requirements. Please write these down, as the website has no way of recording or remembering your results. If you feel your life circumstances have changed, you may want to take the quiz again in the future and see if different needs appear. In general, as you learn to fulfill your top four personal requirements, you'll also get better at fulfilling all the other needs you may have. For a full explanation of personal requirements and emotional needs, please read my book *The Secret Laws of Attraction*. This book fully explains how to get these requirements satisfied so that they do not end up damaging your professional and personal relationships. This is critical knowledge for anyone interested in reaching the upper echelons of senior management or breaking through the glass ceiling.

The Highlands Program (highlandsco.com)

This comprehensive online computerized assessment will help you identify your inherent abilities and will tell you just how introverted or extroverted you are, how far you think into the future, how your brain is hardwired to see the world, whether you have the three elements of musical ability, and lots of other valuable information. Of all the online assessments I have experienced, this one is my favorite for anyone in a career transition or about to embark on an expensive educational or training program. It is well worth the financial investment and time, as it could save you years of time and thousands of dollars spent for the wrong education or training. For more information, or if you are interested in taking this assessment and having a private coaching call and debrief, please e-mail us at info@lifecoach.com.

The Career Planning Insights Report and Workplace Motivators Report

I use both of these online computerized reports with my coaching clients because they are statistically more accurate than the Myers-Briggs program and they take only ten minutes each to complete online. You'll instantly receive a twenty-four-page report that will tell you what your personal style is and your top hidden motivating values—the ones that inform every decision that you make, whether you are aware of them or not. Results are remarkably accurate, but everyone benefits from a debrief session with a qualified coach to fully interpret the results and apply them in life—very useful information for anyone making a career change or starting a business. They are also great tools for team building and can help managers quickly understand how to leverage a team's strengths to get the highest productivity and morale. I've even used these assessments in relationship coaching to help couples and partners better understand and appreciate each other. If you are interested in taking these assessments online, or if you are a manager and would like to use these assessments with your staff, please contact info@lifecoach.com for more information.

StrengthsFinder Profile

There is a handy little strengths assessment in the book *Now, Discover Your Strengths* by Marcus Buckingham and Donald Clifton. Buy this book new, because its main value is the password that you can use to take the online assessment, which will tell you your top five strengths.

Audio Programs

Coach Yourself to Success *Phone Class Led by Talane Miedaner*

This is the recording of a live, nine-week *Coach Yourself to Success* phone class. If you've missed the class or it doesn't fit into your schedule, you can listen to the nine-hour course at your convenience. This phone class covers the essential steps to being successful in all areas of your life. It is designed to be used in conjunction with the book *Coach Yourself to Success* and includes a set of nine-week online coaching assignments in addition to the audio download or CD. If you prefer to be an active participant, sign up for a live phone class at Lifecoach.com.

Irresistible Attraction: A Way of Life *by Talane Miedaner*
This fifty-five-minute audiotape or CD outlines the five basic steps in becoming more attractive to both personal and professional contacts—essential for effective networking and selling. It is only available at Lifecoach.com. Sign up for a free sample week of online coaching and you'll receive this professionally recorded audio download for free!

Subliminal Programs

Alphasonics International
Cuesta Road
Santa Fe, NM 87505
Tel: 505-466-7773 or 800-937-2574

Subliminal programs for all manner of issues from wealth building to stopping sugar addictions. I have used the company's *Attracting Infinite Riches* audio, which suggests such ideas as "I create prosperity; earning money makes me feel good; multiplying money is fun; I am happy about my wealth; rivers of riches are flowing to me." All you will hear is a babbling brook. Contact Alphasonics for more information on how subliminal programs work and for details on all of the company's other titles.

Paraliminal Programs

Learning Strategies Corporation (learningstrategies.com)
Paul Scheele has created a vast number of excellent paraliminal programs to help with topics ranging from anxiety to perfect health. I particularly like the "Sonic Access" programs and use them as a guided meditation—powerful stuff. If you aren't used to meditating, this is a great way to get started. Experts estimate that we are only using a small percentage of our brains. This is one way to expand your brain power effortlessly.

Help Yourself

Childcare International
Trafalgar House
Grenville Place
London NW7 3SA
United Kingdom
Tel: +44-(0)20-8906-3116 or +44-(0)20-8959-3611
Fax: +44-(0)20-8906-3461
E-mail: office@childcareint.co.uk
Web: childint.co.uk

If you think you can't afford live-in child care, think again. For a small weekly stipend plus room and board, you can hire an au pair through an agency. The agency does the background and security checks for you. I have used Childcare International with great results. The company also can provide full-time nannies and caregivers for elderly people. A friend of mine uses Christian Au Pairs at christianaupairs.com with good success.

Professional Resources

National Association of Professional Organizers (napo.net)
4700 W. Lake Avenue
Glenview, IL 60025
Tel: 847-375-4746

If you are struggling to get organized or want to clear the clutter, call this association for a referral to a professional organizer in your area. NAPO offers an e-mail referral service too.

Assist U (assistu.com)
Tel: 866-829-6757 (toll-free)
Contact: Stacy Brice

Free up your time with a virtual assistant to handle administrative tasks. For a referral to a well-trained virtual assistant who will perform administrative, accounting, and other tasks, contact Assist U. This company also trains people to become virtual assistants.

Association of Image Consultants International
Tel: 800-383-8831

Call this number for referrals to professional image consultants in your area. I recommend that you interview a few consultants before making your final choice.

Associated Skin Care Professionals
1271 Sugarbush Drive
Evergreen, CO 80439
Tel: 800-789-0411

Call the ASCP for a skin-care professional in your area.

How to Find or Become a Coach

Here we are at the end of the book, and you probably see a few areas in your life that need some work. It doesn't take forever to attract the career and the life you want. The rewards are well worth the work and start to kick in immediately, so don't wait—start working through the exercises today. If you want to make it easy on yourself, hire a coach to help you through this process and keep you on track.

Finding a Coach

Left to our own devices, we don't progress as quickly. We all have blind spots, and it is helpful to have an outsider point them out. Anyone who has hired a personal trainer knows it is much more fun to go to the gym or do ten push-ups with someone egging you on and keeping an eye on your posture than trying to do it alone. The same goes for a life coach. When you are discouraged and ready to quit, you can count on your coach to be there to keep you going through the tough spots. You can count on your coach to tell you the truth. Your friends and family can't always tell you the truth, because they don't want to risk the relationship or because they have their own agendas in mind.

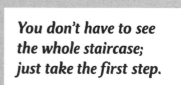

You don't have to see the whole staircase; just take the first step.

—MARTIN LUTHER KING JR.

Here are some pointers on finding an excellent coach:

Hire a professional, someone who has been through a specialized coach-training program, so you know he or she has some basic skills. Plenty of people are suddenly calling themselves coaches when in fact they are therapists, counselors, or consultants and have never completed a real coach-training program.

When you interview the coach, you should feel that you can tell this person the whole truth. Is this a person you can confide in? A person you trust and respect? Do you feel listened to and understood?

As a general rule, do not hire a close friend or a family member, for the reasons already mentioned. You don't want the coaching to affect your relationship. You can always fire your coach, but you can't fire your cousin or uncle. Keep friends and family for love, support, and encouragement.

Does this coach have the experience, skills, and qualifications you are looking for? Don't be afraid to ask to speak to some of the coach's clients for a recommendation, especially clients who had success in the area you want to develop. Ask what is the coach's style and philosophy and whether he or she has any particular coaching specialty. Some coaches specialize in relationships, some in working with creative clients, some with entrepreneurs, people with head injuries—you name it. Whatever your particular need, you are guaranteed that there is a coach out there who specializes in it.

Don't worry about where the coach lives. Most coaches work by telephone, as it is more effective and efficient than in-person meetings. My clients are all over the globe, and most of them I've never met in person. It makes no difference to the results they achieve.

If you aren't having fun and seeing results with your coach, tell your coach what you need from him or her. If that doesn't work, ask for a referral to a different coach. In the first few sessions, you will typically assess your current situation and talk about where you'd like to be. In a corporate setting, you may discuss how the company goals work in relation to your own. You can expect your coach to provide ongoing positive support and encouragement, to ask you to go beyond where you'd normally stop, to press you to try new skills, to provide follow-up discussion on the goals you are working on, and to give you life work assignments every week. It is also perfectly OK to tell your coach how you are best coached. I usually ask my clients this anyway.

Whenever you find yourself getting bogged down or overwhelmed with a project, it is a good idea to find some help, whether that is a tutor to help you decipher a new computer program, a professional organizer to help you get your home in order, or a coach to help you live your dreams and attract everything you've always wanted. You can do this!

Coaching Organizations

International Coach Federation
2365 Harrodsburg Road, Suite A325
Lexington, KY 40504
Tel: 888-423-3131 (toll-free) or 859-219-3580
Fax: 859-226-4411
E-mail: icfheadquarters@coachfederation.org
Web: coachfederation.org

The International Coach Federation (ICF) is the source of information worldwide on one of the fastest-growing professions. The largest worldwide nonprofit professional association of personal and business coaches, the ICF provides coach certification and hosts an annual coaching conference. The federation maintains the standards of training for the coaching industry and provides three levels of coaching certification: ACC (Associate Certified Coach), PCC (Professional Certified Coach), and the highest designation, MCC (Master Certified Coach). If you are looking for a coach-training program, make sure it is, at the very least, approved by the ICF, or you won't qualify for the certification.

The International Coaching Directory
Tel: 407-628-2909
Web: thecoachingdirectory.org

All coaches listed on this international coach referral service are graduates of or in training at an ICF-accredited training program. Try a free half-hour coaching call with any that are available.

Lifecoach.com
Contact: Faye Morgan
4017 Corrine Drive
Orlando, FL 32814
Tel: 407-628-2909 or 888-4-TALANE (toll-free)
E-mail: info@lifecoach.com
Web: Lifecoach.com

Lifecoach.com provides you with the latest in coaching technology and the most highly trained coaches in the world. Your Accredited Life Coach will help you attain the career, business, and life you have always wanted. The company offers the following services:

→ Individual coaching
→ Group coaching
→ Corporate coaching
→ Keynotes and workshops
→ Retreats and seminars designed to meet the needs of your organization or group
→ Monthly phone classes via an internationally accessible teleconference call
→ Online computerized assessments (The Highlands Program; The Career Planning Insights Report; Workplace Motivators)
→ Monthly newsletters
→ Online coaching programs
→ The Emotional Index Quiz
→ The Personal Requirements Quiz

For a free e-mail subscription to *Talane's Coaching Tip of the Week* and/or the quarterly newsletter, send an e-mail to subscribe@lifecoach.com or sign up directly at Lifecoach.com. For a list of upcoming phone classes and events, please go directly to Lifecoach.com or contact our company at the address listed here.

Becoming a Coach

For a complete listing of all the accredited coach-training schools and organizations, please see the International Coach Federation website at coachfederation.org. Programs vary widely in quality and content. My personal recommendation is:

CoachInc.com
Tel: 800-48-COACH
E-mail: admissions@coachinc.com

Attend the free CoachInc.com Question and Answer TeleClass to learn about the programs and services offered by Coach U and Corporate Coach U. Also available is "Becoming a Coach," a four-week course conducted via highly interactive TeleClasses. This course shares valuable information about beginning your own coaching practice and allows you to hear and experience coaching. The Core Essentials program, where everyone begins training, is both challenging and fun and takes approximately fifteen months to complete. New coaches are also encouraged to participate in the Mentor Coach program to find an experienced mentor coach.

The Coaches Training Institute
4000 Civic Center Drive, Suite 500
San Rafael, CA 94903
Tel: 415-451-6000 or 800-691-6008
E-mail: info@thecoaches.com
Web: thecoaches.com

If you would like an admissions adviser to contact you, please use the Contact Us form on the website, and someone will respond within one business day. For general information write to cti-info@thecoaches.com.

Index

About the Author

One of the most widely recognized coaches in the world, Talane Miedaner, author of the international bestseller *Coach Yourself to Success* and *The Secret Laws of Attraction* (McGraw-Hill), is the owner and founder of Lifecoach.com. She has gained international prominence as a life coach by guiding thousands of people to wealth, success, and happiness. As a leader in the cutting-edge field of personal and professional coaching, Talane helps people structure their lives so that they can easily attract the opportunities they want. Her team of coaches works with executives, managers, public officials, entrepreneurs, corporations, and business owners around the world in person, by phone, and online. Talane leads numerous seminars and workshops nationally and internationally and occasionally teaches at Coach U, from which she received certification as a professional coach, and at Georgetown University. She is a member of the International Coach Federation and is a Master Certified Coach. She has also published a number of audio programs, including *Irresistible Attraction: A Way of Life*, as well as a workbook for coaching. Talane is the host of the national radio show "The 60 Second Coach" and has been a regular columnist for *Natural Health* magazine.

Talane holds a degree in both international affairs from the School of Foreign Service and a master's in English from Georgetown University. Prior to becoming a coach, Talane held a corporate position as second vice president at Chase Manhattan Bank in New York. She now spends her time between England and America with her husband and two daughters.

For more information on finding a *Coach Yourself to a New Career* group near you, please join Talane's online community and subscribe to her free weekly coaching tips by visiting her website at Lifecoach.com.

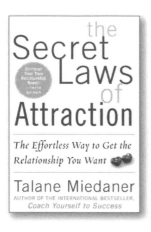